DOCTOR BOWL

DR. DIVYA SHARMA

K

An Hachette UK Company
www.hachette.co.uk

First published in Great Britain in 2022 by
Kyle Books, an imprint of Kyle Cathie Ltd
Carmelite House
50 Victoria Embankment
London EC4Y 0DZ
www.kylebooks.co.uk

ISBN: 9781914239090

Distributed in the US by Hachette Book Group,
1290 Avenue of the Americas,
4th and 5th Floors, New York, NY 10104

Distributed in Canada by Canadian Manda Group,
664 Annette St., Toronto, Ontario, Canada M6S 2C8

Editor: Louise McKeever
Design: Imagist
Photography: Cara Cormack
Food styling: Saskia Sidey
Props styling: Lucy Attwater
Production: Katherine Hockley

A Cataloguing in Publication record for this title is available from the British Library

Printed and bound in China

10 9 8 7 6 5 4 3 2 1

FOR MY DARLING
ANOUSHKA,

YOU CAN BE ANYTHING
YOU WANT TO BE.

LOVE,
YOUR MAMA

Contents

Introduction

Hi, I'm Divya. I'm an NHS GP and a real big foodie, but I'm going to be completely honest with you – I haven't been a keen cook from a young age nor am I a professional chef. However, what I do have are the skills and knowledge that I've accumulated over the years to create quick, wholesome, nutritious and delicious meals. Yes, you've probably read that a thousand times in many different cookbooks, but this book is going to help you lead a healthier lifestyle without spending hours in the kitchen cooking (or cleaning!). You're going to be able to whip up delicious food in no time. You'll also learn about the nutritional benefits of key ingredients to help you understand your food better.

At the age of 31, I had my first child, Anoushka. Being a doctor, everyone around me assumed that I would 'be okay' dealing with motherhood. But wow did it hit me like a truck. The lack of sleep, time and energy was a complete shock to the system. I could see my mental health deteriorate. I tried desperately to do all the things we were taught during GP training to help improve my mood, like exercising and eating well, but trying to find nutritious meals that didn't take hours to make was difficult. So, I started to create my own recipes in the early hours of the morning while I was breastfeeding! The next day, I would look forward to testing out these recipes, and 90 per cent of the time they were a success. After a few months of my husband being the taste-tester, he suggested I should start my own Instagram page and share them with people who might also be struggling to cook with limited time. I was shocked by how popular the page became. Every day I would see more and more people create my recipes and it was such a rewarding feeling.

I want to help you transform your diet with quick, no-fuss, delicious recipes. These are the type of recipes you need when you get home late at night and you can't be bothered to cook – there will be something in this book for you to rustle up in under 30 minutes. All the ingredients are accessible and cheap, so you won't have any recipes that need spirulina powder or anything like that!

All the recipes in this book are also vegan or vegetarian. Plant-based diets are becoming increasingly popular, and they have been shown to have multiple health benefits, such as improving your gut health and reducing your cardiovascular risk. The nutritional information for each recipe is for one serving and almost every recipe can be enjoyed in a bowl, because everything tastes better in a bowl, right?

Divya

KEY

 VEGAN RECIPE

+ VEGAN OPTION AVAILABLE

Keep your kitchen clean and organized

Having to hunt through the cutlery drawer for a garlic crusher is probably where most time is wasted in the kitchen. An organized and clean kitchen will ultimately allow more efficient cooking. Labelling commonly used ingredients like your spices or flours makes it much easier to just grab and go. This also goes for your fridge-freezer.

Know the recipe

Have a good read of the recipe before you start to tackle it. I find this is the most important step to being a fast and efficient cook. Knowing in advance that you'll need a blender or what you'll need to prep in advance is a great time saver. Getting out all the equipment or cutlery you need before you start will save time and reduce stress.

Learn how to multitask

This tip goes hand in hand with the one above. If you understand the steps of the recipe, you'll be able to be three steps ahead. So, if the method calls for roasting some veggies or boiling some pasta, embrace that time and start the next step of the recipe or clean up the kitchen.

Clean as you cook

There's nothing worse than creating a delicious bowl of food but then having to tackle the mess in the kitchen afterward! Cleaning as you cook makes things so much easier and washing up a bowl of melted chocolate straight away is much simpler than once it is hardened. Also, when you cook with clean, uncluttered surfaces it makes things more efficient.

Freeze what you can

Don't underestimate the power of your freezer. It will help you batch-cook meals, keep leftovers and reduce food waste. It can also speed up your recipes massively. For example, I always make big batches of frozen ginger paste and garlic paste so that I have convenient cubes ready to add to recipes without having to make a small amount each time. I simply blend quantities of ginger and garlic (separately) and add the blended mixture to ice cube trays and freeze. Once frozen, pop the cubes out of the tray and store in an airtight container in the freezer. Frozen fruit is great to keep at hand for all kinds of recipes. It is a common misconception that frozen fruit and vegetables have less nutritional value than fresh, but actually they are almost equal in terms of nutritional content.

Sharpen your knives

Having a sharp knife is essential in your kitchen. A dull knife requires more effort and force to cut through ingredients, therefore increasing your risk of harming yourself. Also, when your ingredients are cut with a sharp knife you're more likely to get precise cuts, which will help the food cook more evenly and at the same rate. Plus, it will look nicer in your bowl.

Cut veggies smaller

If you're really short on time, know that cutting your veggies smaller or thinner will mean that you can cook them faster.

Put the music on!

Having my favourite track on in the kitchen gets me in the mood to cook something delicious. It also gets me in the zone and reduces stress!

Most of my recipes don't require any technical or expensive equipment like a stand mixer or any fancy gadgets. However, I have listed some equipment that is essential to allow you to create delicious food in less time.

Blender

A good-quality, high-speed blender is a great piece of equipment to create the soups, dips, desserts and smoothies that are featured in this book. To clean your blender, simply fill the blender with warm water, add one to two drops of washing-up liquid, and blend it at a low speed for about 30 seconds. If you don't have space in your kitchen for a blender, a stick blender is a great option too.

Sharp knife

You'll need a sharp knife to prep most of your ingredients, so it's important to invest in a good-quality one and look after it.

Pans

A stainless-steel saucepan is a great investment for your cooking as it can last you decades. It is great for one-pot meals, which you'll see featured in this book. Other useful additions are a wok and a decent, heavy-based frying pan.

Mixing bowls

For mixing together salad dressings, batters, marinades, sauces and even for storing leftovers, mixing bowls are a must.

Baking sheet

From roasting veggies to baking cookies, a good-quality baking sheet will be used many times in your kitchen.

Chopping board

A decent-sized wooden chopping board will probably be used every time you cook. It doesn't need to cost the earth, and it will last you a lifetime.

Storage containers

Containers are necessary to store your leftovers and also to transport your lunch. I use glass containers as they double up as serving dishes too, saving space in your kitchen. Plus, they are much better for the environment.

It's important to make sure your kitchen is stocked up appropriately. Not only will this help save time, but also help ease the stress of making your meals. Before you head to the supermarket, have a look at what you already have in your kitchen and pantry, and check their expiry dates. You may be surprised that you already have a lot of the key ingredients hiding at the back of your cupboards. It's happened to me too many times before and now I have accumulated about four jars of turmeric!

Herbs and spices

Dried herbs
Oregano
Mixed herbs

Spices
Salt
Pepper
Ground cumin
Ground coriander
Ground turmeric
Garam masala
Chilli powder
Paprika

Fresh aromatics
Chillies
Garlic
Ginger
Fresh herbs

Canned food

Plum tomatoes
Baked beans
Pulses: lentils, chickpeas, kidney
    beans and black beans
Coconut milk

Dried goods

Pasta
Rice: white or brown
Couscous

Quinoa
Noodles
Dried fruit
Rolled oats

Nuts and seeds

Almonds
Walnuts
Cashews
Pistachios
Chia seeds
Flaxseed

Condiments

Oils: extra virgin and light olive oil
Balsamic vinegar
Soy sauce or tamari
Honey
Maple syrup
Mayonnaise
Ketchup

Baking ingredients

Flour: gram, plain and self-raising
Baking powder
Bicarbonate of soda
Cocoa/cacao powder
Sugar
Nut butters

Freezer

Frozen vegetables
Sweetcorn
Peas
Cauliflower
Broccoli

Frozen fruit
Bananas
Berries
Mango

Protein

Tofu
Veggie mince

Bread, flatbread and pitta

Chapter 1

Breakfast

This chapter is all about making exciting, tasty breakfasts that require minimal effort and time. From new ways to make mouthwatering pancakes to indulgent smoothie bowls, on-the-go breakfasts and tofu omelettes, these recipes are sure to brighten up your morning.

Chocolate and peanut butter smoothie ●v

PREP TIME	5 mins
SERVES	2

2 large frozen bananas (peel and
chop the bananas, then freeze)
2 tbsp peanut butter,
    smooth or crunchy
2 tbsp cacao or cocoa powder
1–2 Medjool dates (or you can
    substitute with 2 tbsp maple
    syrup or honey)
4 tbsp almond milk
    (or your milk of choice)

TOPPINGS
banana slices
handful of chopped peanuts
roughly chopped dark chocolate

1— Add all the ingredients to a high-speed blender and blend until thick, smooth and creamy.

2— If you find the smoothie consistency too thick, you can slowly add more milk.

3— Transfer the smoothie to two bowls and add your choice of toppings.

Note — Get in the habit of peeling, chopping and freezing some bananas before they become overripe – that way you'll always have some to hand to make this smoothie.

NUTRITIONAL INFORMATION

Calories	249kcal
Carbohydrates	41.5g
Protein	6.5g
Fat	9.4g
Fibre	7.3g
Sugar	23.5g

NOTE: Excluding the toppings

Carrot and orange smoothie ⓥ

PREP TIME	5 mins
SERVES	1

1 large orange, peeled and
    segmented, with pips removed
1 large carrot,
    peeled and roughly chopped
1 medium banana
100ml (3½fl oz) water
1cm (½ inch) piece
    of fresh ginger, grated
2 tbsp rolled oats
2 tbsp lemon juice
¼ tsp ground turmeric

TOPPINGS (OPTIONAL)
pomegranate seeds
mint
chopped pistachio nuts

1— Place all the ingredients in a high-speed blender and purée until smooth.

2— If it's too thick, slowly add a tablespoon of cold water until you get the desired consistency.

3— Tip into a bowl and serve with your toppings of choice.

NUTRITIONAL INFORMATION

Calories	278kcal
Carbohydrates	62.3g
Protein	5g
Fat	1.4g
Fibre	10.4g
Sugar	35.1g

NOTE: Excluding the toppings

Porridge base v

PREP TIME	5 mins
SERVES	10

300g (10½oz) rolled oats
100g (3½oz) quinoa, uncooked
150g (5½oz) nuts,
    such as almonds, hazelnuts
    or cashews
60g (2¼oz) pumpkin seeds
60g (2¼oz) sunflower seeds

1— First, make your porridge base. Combine all the ingredients together in an airtight container. The dry mix will keep at room temperature for up to 3 months.

Porridge v

COOK TIME	5 mins
SERVES	1

180ml (6½fl oz) almond milk
    (or your milk of choice)
60g (2¼oz) Porridge base
    (see above)

1— To make a single serving of porridge, pour the almond milk into a small saucepan and bring to the boil over a high heat. Pour the porridge base into the boiling milk.

2— Stir to combine, then reduce the heat to low and simmer, uncovered and stirring occasionally, for about 4–5 minutes until the oats have absorbed most of the liquid and are creamy in texture. If it's too dry, you can slowly add more milk to get your preferred consistency.

3— Transfer to a bowl and serve with one of the following toppings.

NUTRITIONAL INFORMATION

Calories	328kcal
Carbohydrates	32g
Protein	10.5g
Fat	18.5g
Fibre	5.9g
Sugar	2.2g

Caramelized pears with crushed pecans + ⓥ

PREP TIME	5 mins
COOK TIME	10 mins
SERVES	2

1 tbsp butter
    (use non-dairy butter if vegan)
½ tbsp brown sugar
1 large pear, peeled,
    cored and roughly chopped
1 tbsp lemon juice
¼ tsp ground cinnamon
50g (1¾oz) pecans, crushed

1— Heat a small saucepan over a medium heat. Once hot, add the butter.

2— As soon as the butter is bubbling, add the brown sugar and stir. Now add the pear, lemon juice and cinnamon and stir to coat.

3— Cover to steam and soften the pear and cook for 5–6 minutes or until tender and golden brown.

4— Once tender, remove the lid to allow the pear to caramelize for a few minutes.

5— Top your porridge with the pear and sprinkle over the crushed pecans.

NUTRITIONAL INFORMATION

Calories	266kcal
Carbohydrates	15.4g
Protein	2.6g
Fat	23.7g
Fibre	4.7g
Sugar	8.7g

Warm berry compote

PREP TIME	2 mins
COOK TIME	8 mins
SERVES	1

50g (1¾oz) berry mix,
    frozen or fresh
½ tsp ground cinnamon,
    plus extra to serve
1 tsp maple syrup,
    plus extra to drizzle
handful of pistachios, crushed

1— Put the berries, cinnamon and maple syrup in a small saucepan over a medium heat. Cook for 8 minutes, stirring occasionally, until piping hot and the fruit has started to break down and the liquid is syrupy.

2— Top your porridge with the compote, drizzle maple syrup over and scatter with some crushed pistachios and a pinch of cinnamon.

NUTRITIONAL INFORMATION

Calories	303kcal
Carbohydrates	21.6g
Protein	9.8g
Fat	21.2g
Fibre	7.3g
Sugar	11.1g

Tofu omelette with guacamole ⓥ

PREP TIME	10 mins
COOK TIME	10 mins
SERVES	2

OMELETTE
350g (12oz) silken tofu, drained
2 garlic cloves, finely chopped
70g (2½oz) gram (chickpea) flour
1 tbsp cornflour
2 tbsp nutritional yeast
2 tbsp olive oil
½ tsp ground turmeric
½ tsp kala namak (black salt)
    or 1 tsp salt
pepper

GUACAMOLE
3 very ripe medium avocados
1 large ripe tomato, finely chopped
juice of 1 large lime
handful of fresh coriander,
    finely chopped
1 small red onion, finely chopped
1 red or green chilli, finely chopped
salt and pepper

1— Add all the tofu omelette ingredients to a blender and purée until smooth. Make sure you scrape down the sides so that everything is well incorporated.

2— Preheat a large non-stick frying pan over a medium–high heat. Lightly grease with either cooking spray or a very thin layer of oil.

3— Once hot, pour half the batter into the pan to create an 18cm (7 inch) circle.

4— Cover and cook for 3–5 minutes, checking often to see if it's done. When the edges have dried out and the middle is no longer liquid, lift a small section with a spatula and check to see that the omelette is set.

5— While the omelette is cooking, make your guacamole. Cut the avocados in half and remove the stones. Using a spoon, remove the flesh and place into a bowl. Add the rest of the ingredients into the bowl and mix well. Season with salt and pepper.

6— When the omelette is ready, loosen by sliding the spatula under it from each direction, and then fold one side over the other.

7— Cook for about 1 more minute and then repeat the above with the remaining batter.

8— Serve the omelettes topped with the guacamole.

NUTRITIONAL INFORMATION

Calories	491kcal
Carbohydrates	38g
Protein	17.2g
Fat	32.1g
Fibre	13.1g
Sugar	8.9g

Coffee

Whizz with coconut oil for a bullet-proof coffee. Try with different plant-based milks in a cappuccino. Or add a shot to your cocoa-based smoothie bowls and breakfast bars.

Statistics show that coffee is the second most-consumed beverage after water. It contains good amounts of vitamins B2, B5 and traceable amounts of magnesium and manganese. Its high caffeine content also helps to improve physical performance and increase alertness, energy and concentration – so much so that it's used by some athletes to improve endurance.

However, the high caffeine content seems to be a double-edged sword. Always remember that moderation is key as everyone reacts differently to caffeine. One mug of instant coffee contains around 100mg of caffeine.

Coffee can favourably affect blood-sugar balance in some people, thanks to the effect caffeine has on glucose absorption from carbohydrate-high foods. This in turn slows down the transition of glucose into the bloodstream, stabilizing levels in the blood. Coffee can also boost fat burning and the body's metabolism. A lesser-known fact is that it is also high in antioxidants, namely chlorogenic acid and caffeic acid, which directly increase antioxidant levels in the blood.

Coffee can help with cognitive function. This is due to its ability to cause vasodilation, leading to increased blood flow to the brain. This, coupled with its antioxidant properties, could offer protection for neurological conditions, such as Alzheimer's and Parkinson's disease. Linked to this also is coffee's ability to increase cognitive performance thanks to its role in aiding neurogenesis (creating new neurons in the brain).

On the negative side, coffee can cause digestive problems for some as it can damage the gut microbiome in those susceptible. It can also cause reflux and leave some individuals feeling jittery and anxious and cause disturbed sleep. If you can tolerate coffee, always remember to drink extra water alongside each cup as it is a diuretic and can leave you feeling dehydrated.

Creamy mocha smoothie bowl ⓥ

PREP TIME	5 mins
SERVES	1

100ml (3½fl oz) brewed coffee,
    cooled in the fridge
1 frozen medium-ripe banana
1 tbsp peanut butter
    (or your nut butter of choice)
70g (2½oz) frozen cauliflower
4 tbsp oat milk
    (or your milk of choice)
½ tbsp cacao powder

1— Put all the ingredients in a high-speed blender and purée until smooth.

2— If the smoothie is too thick, slowly add cold water, a tablespoon at a time, until you get the desired consistency.

3— Transfer the smoothie to a bowl.

NUTRITIONAL INFORMATION

Calories	261kcal
Carbohydrates	42.9g
Protein	8.6g
Fat	9.5g
Fibre	9.4g
Sugar	21.9g

Quinoa granola ⓥ

PREP TIME	5 mins
COOK TIME	30 mins
SERVES	5

90g (3¼oz) rolled oats
90g (3¼oz) quinoa, uncooked
75g (2½oz) any nuts, chopped
2 tbsp chia seeds
1 tsp ground cinnamon
pinch salt
3 tbsp coconut oil, melted
3 tbsp maple syrup
25g (1oz) toasted coconut flakes

1— Preheat the oven to 160°C (325°F), Gas Mark 3 and line a baking sheet with parchment paper.

2— Add the oats, quinoa, nuts, chia seeds, cinnamon and salt to a mixing bowl and stir to combine. Add the oil and maple syrup and stir well. If the mixture is too dry, slowly add more maple syrup.

3— Spread in an even layer on your baking sheet.

4— Bake on the middle rack of the oven for 25 minutes and then sprinkle with coconut flakes and bake for a further 5 minutes.

5— Remove and allow to cool.

NUTRITIONAL INFORMATION

Calories	371kcal
Carbohydrates	39.4g
Protein	8.9g
Fat	21.1g
Fibre	6.5g
Sugar	9.5g

Notes — Why not double or even triple the ingredients, to make a bigger batch? You just need to store it in an airtight container for up to 2 weeks, or it can be frozen for up to 1 month.

If you avoid nuts or don't have any to hand, granola is equally good made with dried fruit, such as raisins

Overnight granola and apple jars ⓥ

PREP TIME	5 mins
CHILLING TIME	8 hours
SERVES	2

250g (9oz) coconut yogurt
(or your yogurt of choice)
150g (5½oz) granola (see page 27)
1 small Granny Smith apple (or your
apple of choice), coarsely grated
¼ tsp ground cinnamon

TOPPINGS
grated apple
handful of flaked almonds
maple syrup

1— Add all the ingredients to a large bowl and mix until well coated.

2— Divide this mixture into two small jars or pots.

3— Cover and refrigerate for at least 8 hours, but no longer than 3 days.

4— Top with some additional grated apple, flaked almonds and a drizzle of maple syrup.

NUTRITIONAL INFORMATION

Calories	653kcal
Carbohydrates	90.7g
Protein	15.6g
Fat	28.2g
Fibre	12.2g
Sugar	42.5g

Overnight chocolate orange chia pots Ⓥ

PREP TIME	5 mins
CHILLING TIME	8 hours
SERVES	4

120g (4oz) rolled oats
250ml (9fl oz) almond milk
   (or your milk of choice)
2 tbsp maple syrup
2 tbsp cacao powder
2 tbsp chia seeds
zest and juice of ½ medium orange

TOPPINGS
100g (3½oz) coconut yogurt
   (or your yogurt of choice)
½ medium orange, segmented
handful of dark chocolate chips

1— Put all the ingredients in a bowl and mix until well combined.

2— Pour the oat mixture into four jars or bowls. Cover with lids and place in the refrigerator to chill for 8 hours or overnight.

3— To serve, stir the oats and top with a layer of yogurt, orange segments and chocolate chips.

NUTRITIONAL INFORMATION

Calories	394kcal
Carbohydrates	40.9g
Protein	6.9g
Fat	12.3g
Fibre	7.8g
Sugar	11.8g

Granola
yogurt cups Ⓥ

PREP TIME	10 mins
COOK TIME	15 mins
SERVES	9

150g (5½oz) rolled oats
25g (1oz) desiccated coconut
½ tsp ground cinnamon
3 tbsp maple syrup
2 tbsp smooth peanut
    or almond butter
18 tbsp coconut yogurt
    (or your yogurt of choice)
fruits of your choice

1— Preheat the oven to 160°C (325°F), Gas Mark 3. Lightly grease nine muffin cups in a muffin tin.

2— Put your rolled oats, coconut and ground cinnamon in a bowl and mix together.

3— Put the maple syrup and nut butter in a small pan over a low heat. Whisk together until warm and both ingredients are runny and have combined.

4— Add the nut butter mixture to the oat mixture and stir well to combine. The mixture should come together. If it is too dry, you can slowly add more maple syrup.

5— Divide the mixture evenly among the nine muffin cups. Using your fingers, press the oat mixture into the bottom and up the sides of each muffin cup, to make a cup shape.

6— Bake for 15 minutes or until the edges are golden brown.

7— Let the granola cups to cool completely in the muffin tin. Once cooled, carefully remove using a round-bladed knife.

8— Fill each cup with 2 tbsp of yogurt and top with your favourite fruits.

NUTRITIONAL INFORMATION

Calories	127kcal
Carbohydrates	17.6g
Protein	3.1g
Fat	4.9g
Fibre	2.4g
Sugar	5.1g

NOTE: Excluding the fruit

Notes— Instead of fresh fruit you can top with some frozen fruit.

To save time, you can make the granola cups in advance and store in the refrigerator for up to 3 days or freeze them for up to 3 months. Then when you're ready to serve, thaw the granola cups and fill with your desired fillings.

Coffee baked oats + ⓥ

PREP TIME	10 mins
COOK TIME	25 mins
SERVES	6

300g (10½oz) rolled oats
1 tsp baking powder
¼ tsp salt
50g (1¾oz) coconut sugar
    or brown sugar
150ml (5fl oz) strong brewed coffee
200ml (7fl oz) almond milk
    (or your milk of choice)
1 egg or 1 flaxseed egg
1 tsp vanilla extract
90g (3¼oz) chocolate chips
2 tbsp hazelnuts, halved

TOPPINGS
yogurt
fruit or berries
maple syrup

1— Preheat the oven to 190°C (375°F), Gas Mark 5. Grease or line a 20cm (8 inch) square baking dish.

2— Combine the oats, baking powder, salt and sugar in a medium bowl and mix well.

3— Add the coffee, milk, egg and vanilla extract and stir to combine.

4— Fold in the chocolate chips, reserving a few to sprinkle on top.

5— Spread in the baking dish, sprinkle with the remaining chocolate chips and hazelnuts and bake for 25 minutes.

6— Serve with yogurt, fruit or berries and a drizzle of maple syrup.

NUTRITIONAL INFORMATION

Calories	337kcal
Carbohydrates	54.8g
Protein	8.8g
Fat	10.5g
Fibre	6.4g
Sugar	19.5g

Super berry smoothie ⓥ

PREP TIME	5 mins
SERVES	1

120g (4oz) frozen berry mix
   (strawberries, blueberries
   and raspberries)
20g (¾oz) rolled oats
2 tbsp coconut yogurt
   (or your yogurt of choice)
1 tbsp chia seeds
1 tbsp maple syrup or agave syrup
   (or honey if not vegan)
350ml (12fl oz) oat milk
   (or your milk of choice)

TOPPINGS (OPTIONAL)
strawberries
chia seeds
toasted coconut flakes

1— Put all the ingredients in a high-speed blender and purée until smooth.

2— If it's too thick, slowly add cold water, a tablespoon at a time, until you get the desired consistency.

3— Serve in a bowl with your choice of toppings.

NUTRITIONAL INFORMATION

Calories	471kcal
Carbohydrates	91.8g
Protein	9.3g
Fat	9.4g
Fibre	13.2g
Sugar	51.5g

NOTE: Excluding the toppings

Chapter 2

Weekend brunch

Ease into your weekend with some restaurant-worthy brunch recipes, which can be thrown together in no time. Enjoy some fiery tofu scramble, crowd-pleasing cauliflower steaks or a selection of toast toppers. These brunch recipes are guaranteed to tantalize your taste buds.

Mexican
tofu scramble ⓥ

PREP TIME	25 mins
DRAINING TIME	15 mins
COOK TIME	20 mins
SERVES	4

NUTRITIONAL INFORMATION

Calories	284kcal
Carbohydrates	31.8g
Protein	20g
Fat	10.1g
Fibre	10g
Sugar	7.5g

NOTE: Excluding the sourdough and toppings

400g (14oz) extra-firm tofu, drained
½ tbsp olive oil
1 small red onion, finely chopped
1 red pepper, deseeded and diced
1 tbsp tomato purée
3 garlic cloves, minced
1 tsp ground coriander
½ tsp ground cumin
½ tsp chilli powder
¼ tsp ground turmeric
2 tbsp nutritional yeast
150g (5½oz) frozen sweetcorn
400g (14oz) can of black beans,
    rinsed and drained
1 vegetable stock cube,
    dissolved in 2 tbsp boiling water
salt and pepper

FLAVOURINGS (OPTIONAL)
3 spring onions, thinly sliced
1 red or green chilli, finely chopped
handful of chopped fresh coriander

TO SERVE (OPTIONAL)
sourdough toast
wedges of avocado
cherry tomatoes
lime wedges

1— Cover the tofu with some
    kitchen paper, and then press
    it down with a heavy object for
    15 minutes to get rid of the
    excess water.

2— Heat the olive oil in a large
    frying pan over a low heat.
    Add the red onion and cook for
    about 5 minutes, until the onion
    is soft.

3— Add the diced red pepper,
    tomato purée and garlic. Cook
    for about 5 more minutes until
    the vegetables are soft.

4— Stir in the ground coriander,
    cumin, chilli and turmeric and
    cook for another minute or two,
    stirring often.

5— When the tofu is ready, use
    your hands to crumble it in
    pieces into the pan, along with
    the nutritional yeast, sweetcorn,
    black beans, vegetable stock
    and some salt and pepper.

6— Cook for about 8 minutes,
    stirring often, until everything
    is heated through. Toward the
    end of cooking, add the spring
    onion, chilli and coriander,
    if using.

7— Serve with toast and your
    choice of avocado, cherry
    tomatoes and wedges of lime.

Smoky BBQ beans and quesadillas + Ⓥ

PREP TIME	10 mins
COOK TIME	25 mins
SERVES	4

BEANS
1 tbsp olive oil
½ red onion, finely chopped
2 garlic cloves, minced
1 small red pepper, finely chopped
1 tbsp tomato purée
2 tbsp BBQ sauce
¼ tsp smoked paprika
¼ tsp chilli powder
1 tbsp light brown sugar
400g (14oz) can of cannellini,
    kidney or pinto beans,
    rinsed and drained
100g (3½oz) passata
salt and pepper

QUESADILLAS
4 tortilla wraps
handful of grated cheese
    (or replace with vegan cheese)
handful of chopped fresh coriander

1— Heat the olive oil in a saucepan over a medium heat. Add the onion and garlic and stir until the onion is translucent and soft, about 5–7 minutes. Add the red pepper and cook for a further 5 minutes.

2— Add the tomato purée, BBQ sauce, smoked paprika, chilli powder and sugar and stir them into the onion. Cook for a further 2 minutes.

3— Add the beans to the pan and give them a good stir so that they're covered in the sauce. Cook for another 2–3 minutes.

4— Pour the passata into the pan and let it simmer until the sauce has thickened, about 5 minutes. Season to taste.

5— Meanwhile, heat a frying pan over a medium heat. Place one tortilla in the pan and top with cheese and coriander. Top with a second tortilla and fry for 1–2 minutes until the base is crisp. Using a spatula, carefully flip the quesadilla and fry for a further 1–2 minutes until piping hot and the cheese has melted. Transfer to a plate and keep warm while you repeat with the remaining tortillas. Cut into wedges and serve with the bowl of smoky beans.

NUTRITIONAL INFORMATION

Calories	152kcal
Carbohydrates	22.9g
Protein	5.5g
Fat	4.6g
Fibre	4.9g
Sugar	8.1g

Cauliflower steaks with chimichurri ⓥ

PREP TIME	15 mins
COOK TIME	35 mins
SERVES	2

CAULIFLOWER STEAKS
1 medium head of cauliflower
2–3 tbsp olive oil
salt and pepper

CHIMICHURRI
50g (1¾oz) fresh coriander,
    finely chopped
50g (1¾oz) fresh parsley,
    finely chopped
3 garlic cloves, finely chopped
1 small red onion, finely diced
1 red chilli, deseeded and finely
    chopped, or ½ tsp chilli flakes
5 tbsp extra virgin olive oil
3 tbsp lemon juice
2 tbsp white wine vinegar
salt

1— To make the chimichurri, put the herbs, garlic, onion and chilli in a bowl.

2— Pour in the oil, lemon juice and vinegar and add salt. Mix together.

3— Allow to sit for 5–10 minutes to release all of the flavours into the oil before using.

4— Preheat the oven to 200°C (400°F), Gas Mark 6 and line a baking tray with parchment paper.

5— Remove and reserve the outer green leaves from the head of cauliflower and trim the stem. Using a large knife, cut the cauliflower in half from top to bottom. Cut a 4cm (1½ inch) thick steak from each half. If the head is large, carefully cut one more steak from each of the cut sides. Any excess cauliflower florets can still be used for this recipe or saved for another recipe.

6— Rub each steak with 2 tbsp of the olive oil, salt and pepper, place onto the prepared tray and roast for 15 minutes. Gently turn over each steak and drizzle over the remaining olive oil. Roast until tender and golden, about 15–20 minutes more. In the last 5 minutes of roasting, add the cauliflower leaves.

7— Top the cauliflower with the chimichurri sauce.

NUTRITIONAL INFORMATION

Calories	523 kcal
Carbohydrates	21g
Protein	7.5g
Fat	48g
Fibre	8g
Sugar	7.5g

Note — Chimichurri is versatile – it makes a great dressing for pasta salads, drizzle on top of pizzas or use as a sandwich spread. Make a big batch and store it in the fridge for up to 2–3 weeks or in the freezer for up to 3 months.

Salt-and-pepper mushrooms on toast + Ⓥ

PREP TIME	5 mins
COOK TIME	15 mins
SERVES	4

1 tbsp sesame or olive oil
300g (10½oz) mushrooms,
    thinly sliced
1 onion, sliced
½ red pepper, deseeded and sliced
½ green pepper,
    deseeded and sliced
4 garlic cloves, minced
3 red chillies, sliced
3 spring onions, sliced
1 tsp salt
1 tsp pepper
2 tbsp rice vinegar
handful of fresh coriander, chopped

TO SERVE
buttered sourdough toast (use
    non-dairy butter if vegan)

1— In a large wok, heat the oil, add the mushrooms and fry for around
    5 minutes. Remove from the pan and set aside.

2— Add the onion and peppers to the wok and stir-fry for a few minutes
    until soft.

3— Add the garlic, chilli and spring onions.

4— Stir until the onion has turned slightly golden, then add salt and pepper.

5— Add the mushrooms back into the pan along with the rice vinegar.
    Stir for a few more minutes and then serve with some toasted buttered
    sourdough. Top with coriander.

NUTRITIONAL INFORMATION

Calories	82kcal
Carbohydrates	10.5g
Protein	3.7g
Fat	3.9g
Fibre	2.6g
Sugar	4.1g

NOTE: Excluding the toast

Note — You can replace the mushrooms with asparagus, broccoli
or cauliflower, but cooking times will vary.

Lentil and sweet potato fritters ⓥ

PREP TIME	15 mins
COOK TIME	30 mins
SERVES	4

190g (6½oz) uncooked red lentils
700ml (1¼ pints) water
1 large sweet potato,
    peeled and grated
2 medium carrots, grated
2 tbsp finely chopped
    fresh coriander
1 small red onion, chopped
2 garlic cloves, minced
1 tsp paprika
100g (3½oz) plain flour
1 tbsp olive oil
salt and pepper

1— Cook the lentils in the water over a medium heat for about 10–12 minutes or until cooked. Drain them after cooking.

2— While the lentils are cooking, use your hands to squeeze out as much water as possible from the grated potato and carrots.

3— In a large bowl, combine the lentils, sweet potato, carrot, coriander, onion, garlic, paprika, salt, pepper and flour. Mix with your hands to incorporate. If the mixture is too moist, gradually add more flour.

4— Use your hands to form patties.

5— Heat the olive oil in a frying pan over medium heat and cook the patties on both sides until golden brown. You can also bake them at 190°C (375°F), Gas Mark 5 for 20–25 minutes, flipping halfway through.

NUTRITIONAL INFORMATION

Calories	362kcal
Carbohydrates	65.6g
Protein	15.9g
Fat	4.5g
Fibre	8.8g
Sugar	5.4g

Mega vegan breakfast traybake ⓥ

PREP TIME	10 mins
COOK TIME	40 mins
SERVES	2

1 large sweet potato, peeled and
　　cut into small chunks
3 garlic cloves, finely chopped
2 tbsp chopped fresh rosemary
½ tsp salt
½ tsp pepper
1 tbsp olive oil
100g (3½oz) on-the-vine
　　cherry tomatoes
150g (5½oz) chestnut mushrooms
4 vegan sausages
400g (14oz) can of baked beans
150g (5½oz) spinach leaves

1— Preheat the oven to 200°C (400°F), Gas Mark 6. Line a baking tray with
　　parchment paper.

2— Put the sweet potato, garlic, rosemary, salt, pepper and ½ tbsp olive oil
　　in a large bowl and mix well.

3— Place the sweet potato and tomatoes on a large baking tray.
　　Bake for 15 minutes.

4— Add the mushrooms and sausages to the baking tray, drizzle with
　　the remaining olive oil and roast for 20 minutes.

5— Add the beans and spinach to the baking tray and roast for
　　a final 5 minutes.

NUTRITIONAL INFORMATION

Calories	580kcal
Carbohydrates	100g
Protein	31g
Fat	9.4g
Fibre	28g
Sugar	23.8g

Avocados

Steam, sauté or roast. Smash on toast with lime and chilli, slice into salads, whizz in smoothies or use to enrich chocolate desserts.

Nutritious, versatile and delicious, avocados are a powerhouse of nutrition and another 'superfood'. A nutrient-dense food, with one half of the fruit counting toward your five-a-day, avocados are a great source of healthy fats, fibre, vitamins A, C, E, K and B6, as well as nutrients often lacking in many diets, such as potassium and magnesium. Potassium is a mineral that helps control the balance of fluids in the body and also helps the heart muscle work properly – it is essential that we have enough potassium in our diet and avocados actually contain twice as much as a banana! Both potassium and magnesium contribute to healthy blood pressure and nervous system function. Carotenoids (vitamin A) and tocopherols (vitamin E) are linked to a reduced risk of cancer. Fibre, as well being great for your bowels, contributes to healthy bacterial diversity in the gut. Good gut health is increasingly being linked to the prevention of many diseases.

A rich source of anti-inflammatory monounsaturated fats (oleic acid) and a smaller amount of polyunsaturated fats, avocados are incredibly heart healthy. These fats promote good levels of cholesterol and a diet rich in them will often replace the addictive processed fats that are associated with heart disease. Plus, perhaps surprisingly, stocking up on these calorie-dense yet filling fruits can be useful for weight loss as they are difficult to over-consume and will keep you feeling fuller for longer.

Avocados also contain antioxidants that are especially beneficial for eye and brain health, such as lutein and zeaxanthin. These may lower your risk of age-related macular degeneration (AMD) and cataracts, as well as neurodegenerative diseases, such as Alzheimer's and dementia. This antioxidant content will also offer protection against oxidative damage from toxins and inflammation.

Smashed chickpeas with harissa yogurt + Ⓥ

PREP TIME	10 mins
COOK TIME	10 mins
SERVES	2

½ tbsp olive oil
½ red onion, finely chopped
2 garlic cloves, minced
400g (14oz) can of chickpeas,
    rinsed and drained
100g (3½oz) Greek yogurt
    (or your yogurt of choice)
3 tsp harissa paste, to taste
2 tbsp chopped fresh coriander
salt and pepper

TO SERVE
sourdough toast
handful of roughly chopped
    fresh coriander
handful of pomegranate seeds

1— In a frying pan, heat the olive oil over a medium heat. Sauté the onion for a few minutes and then add garlic and cook for a further minute. Add in the chickpeas with salt and pepper and cook for 5 minutes. Using a fork, press down on the chickpeas to lightly smash them.

2— Combine the yogurt and harissa paste and season with salt, if desired.

3— Spread the harissa yogurt on toast and top with the chickpeas. Sprinkle over your coriander and pomegranate seeds.

NUTRITIONAL INFORMATION

Calories	350kcal
Carbohydrates	50g
Protein	13.6g
Fat	10.5g
Fibre	9.75g
Sugar	10.5g

NOTE: Excluding the toast

Avocado and pea hummus ⓥ

PREP TIME	5 mins
COOK TIME	5 mins
SERVES	6

150g (5½oz) fresh or frozen peas
1 ripe avocado,
    peeled and stone removed
2 garlic cloves, peeled
2 tbsp tahini
4 tbsp olive oil
2 tbsp cold water
juice of ½ lemon
2 tbsp roughly chopped
    fresh coriander

TO SERVE
your choice of bread

1— Boil the peas in lightly salted water for 3–4 minutes, then refresh under cool water and drain well. Transfer to a high-speed blender. Add the remaining ingredients and blend until smooth.

2— Serve with your choice of warm bread.

NUTRITIONAL INFORMATION

Calories	160kcal
Carbohydrates	7.4g
Protein	3g
Fat	14.1g
Fibre	3.1g
Sugar	1.7g

NOTE: Excluding the toast

Chapter 3

Summer salads

In this chapter you'll find recipes inspired by cuisines all over the world, from Thai to Indian and Moroccan to Chinese. These recipes are perfect for your picnic, lunchbox or BBQ. All of them can be prepared in under 15 minutes with minimal fuss, but maximum taste guaranteed.

Pad Thai salad ⓥ

PREP TIME	15 mins
COOK TIME	15 mins
SERVES	4

PEANUT DRESSING
120g (4oz) smooth peanut butter
75ml (2½fl oz) soy sauce or tamari
3 tbsp lime juice
3 tbsp maple syrup
3 tbsp sriracha (you can omit if you
    don't like hot sauce)
2 garlic cloves
1½ tbsp minced peeled fresh ginger

SALAD
300g (10½oz) Pad Thai rice noodles
225g (8oz) red cabbage, finely sliced
2 large carrots, finely sliced
1 small red pepper,
    deseeded and sliced
small bunch of fresh coriander,
    chopped
15 fresh basil leaves
4 spring onions, sliced

TOPPINGS
3 tbsp roughly chopped peanuts
1 tbsp sesame seeds

1— Add all of the peanut dressing ingredients to a blender and blend until smooth. If the dressing is too thick, you can add 1–2 tbsp of water to thin it. Transfer to a large bowl.

2— Cook the noodles according to the packet directions. Drain and cool.

3— Add the noodles to the bowl of dressing, along with the cabbage, carrot, red pepper, coriander, basil and spring onion.

4— Gently toss to combine. Garnish with chopped peanuts, sesame seeds and lime wedges. Serve immediately.

NUTRITIONAL INFORMATION

Calories	633kcal
Carbohydrates	91g
Protein	18g
Fat	23g
Fibre	7.8g
Sugar	18.8g

Note— You can top this salad with some crispy tofu.

Rainbow orzo salad + Ⓥ

PREP TIME	5 mins
COOK TIME	10 mins
SERVES	4

350g (12oz) orzo pasta
   or any tiny pasta shapes
200g (7oz) rocket or baby spinach
1 cucumber, chopped
150g (5½oz) tomatoes, chopped
400g (14oz) can of chickpeas,
   rinsed and drained
20g (¾oz) fresh basil, chopped
75g (2½oz) feta cheese, crumbled
   (if vegan, replace with vegan
   feta cheese)
½ red onion, diced

BALSAMIC DRESSING
4 tbsp olive oil
2 tbsp lemon juice
1 tbsp balsamic vinegar
1 tsp honey or maple syrup
1 garlic clove, crushed
salt and pepper

1— Cook the orzo according to the packet instructions.

2— While the pasta is cooking, make the dressing. Put all the balsamic dressing ingredients in a small bowl and whisk together (or shake in a lidded jar). Set aside.

3— Drain the orzo in a colander and rinse well with cold water. Tip into a large bowl.

4— Add the rocket, cucumber, tomato, chickpeas, basil, feta and red onion.

5— Drizzle the dressing over the salad and stir again. Taste and add salt and pepper if needed.

NUTRITIONAL INFORMATION

Calories	619kcal
Carbohydrates	89.3g
Protein	21g
Fat	22.1g
Fibre	10.5g
Sugar	9.5g

Crushed cucumber salad ⓥ

PREP TIME	5 mins
RESTING TIME	20 minutes
SERVES	2

1 long cucumber
¾ tsp salt
handful of fresh coriander,
    finely chopped
1 tbsp sesame seeds, toasted
1 tbsp finely chopped red onion

DRESSING
1½ tbsp rice vinegar
2 tsp sesame oil
1½ tsp grated peeled fresh ginger
2 tsp soy sauce
½ tsp sugar
1 red chilli, finely chopped

1— On a chopping board, hold a large knife flat against the cucumber and smash it lightly with your other hand. The cucumber should crack open and smash into four sections. Repeat along its full length. Once the whole cucumber is completely open, cut into bite-sized pieces.

2— Place in a large bowl, sprinkle with salt, toss and let it rest for 20 minutes.

3— Drain the excess liquid from the bowl.

4— Put all the dressing ingredients in a small bowl and whisk together (or shake in a lidded jar).

5— Drizzle the dressing over the cucumber and sprinkle with coriander, sesame seeds and red onion. Toss and serve immediately.

NUTRITIONAL INFORMATION

Calories	89kcal
Carbohydrates	7.5g
Protein	1.8g
Fat	6.7g
Fibre	2.4g
Sugar	3.8g

Mango salsa ⓥ

PREP TIME	5 mins
SERVES	4

3 ripe mangoes,
     stone removed and flesh diced
1 red pepper, deseeded and diced
1 red onion, finely chopped
large bunch of fresh coriander,
     finely chopped
1 green chilli or 1 tsp paprika
juice of 1 large lime
½ tsp salt

TO SERVE
tortilla chips
lime

1— In a large bowl, combine the mango, red pepper, red onion, coriander and chilli. Drizzle with the lime juice.

2— Using a large spoon, stir all the ingredients together.

3— Season to taste with salt, then stir again.

4—Serve with tortilla chips and lime.

NUTRITIONAL INFORMATION

Calories	177kcal
Carbohydrates	43g
Protein	3.2g
Fat	1.2g
Fibre	5.7g
Sugar	37.5g

NOTE: Excluding the tortilla chips

Note— You can use a bag of frozen mango chunks for this. Defrost, drain any juices then cut the chunks into small dice.

Cauliflower

As a cooking ingredient cauliflower is so wonderfully versatile! You can eat the florets and the leaves raw and dipped in hummus or make roasted cauliflower chips. It's a tasty addition to any curry/casserole or stir-fry. It also makes great 'rice' and creamy mash, when mixed with some beans and olive oil.

The everyday cauliflower is a powerhouse of nutrients and actually contains pretty much every vitamin and mineral that we need in our diets. It is high in vitamins C, K and B6, folate, pantothenic acid, potassium, magnesium, manganese and phosphorus – pretty impressive! It is also very low in fat and carbs, which makes it very useful as part of a weight loss/blood-sugar balancing plan. Cauliflower is a source of choline, an essential nutrient we need for mood, memory and recall. And not only is the cauliflower a nutritious powerhouse, the leaves are too.

As with most vegetables, cauliflower is a good source of fibre, which can aid motility and feeds beneficial bacteria to create a healthy microbiome in the gut. Antioxidants are a big feature, too. Most veggies have these in varying amounts but what sets cauliflower apart is that as part of the brassica family (which also includes broccoli, radish, pak choy), it contains an antioxidant called sulforaphane, which plays a role in keeping our heart healthy and is also incredibly beneficial for liver detoxification. This includes healthy oestrogen metabolism, so is especially beneficial for women.

Stuffed avocados + Ⓥ

PREP TIME	5 mins
SERVES	6

3 ripe avocados,
    halved and stone removed
½ cucumber, diced
1 red pepper, deseeded and diced
1 jalapeño pepper or green chilli,
    deseeded and diced
juice of 1 lemon
½ red onion, diced
1 garlic clove, crushed
handful of cherry tomatoes, diced
100g canned sweetcorn,
    rinsed and drained
4 tbsp garlic aïoli
    (you can substitute with
    mayonnaise or hummus)
salt and pepper

1— Put the cucumber, red pepper, jalapeño, lemon juice, red onion, garlic, tomatoes and corn in a mixing bowl. Add the garlic aïoli and mix well until it all comes together.

2— Fill the prepared avocados with the filling and season to taste.

NUTRITIONAL INFORMATION

Calories	115kcal
Carbohydrates	7.1g
Protein	1.3g
Fat	9.6g
Fibre	3.2g
Sugar	1.8g

Tofu tikka salad + Ⓥ

PREP TIME	30 mins
DRAINING TIME	15 mins
COOK TIME	15 mins
CHILLING TIME (OPTIONAL)	1 hour
SERVES	4

TOFU
280g (10oz) extra-firm tofu, drained
2 tsp grated garlic
1 tsp ginger paste (bought or fresh)
1 tsp chilli powder
1 tsp ground coriander
1 tsp ground cumin
1 tsp garam masala
2 tsp Greek yogurt (or substitute with a dairy-free yogurt)
½ tsp white vinegar
2 tbsp gram (chickpea) or plain flour
1 tsp salt
4 tsp vegetable oil

SALAD
170g (6oz) salad leaves
½ red onion, thinly sliced
handful of cherry tomatoes, halved
juice of ½ lemon

NUTRITIONAL INFORMATION

Calories	151kcal
Carbohydrates	8.2g
Protein	10.5g
Fat	8.8g
Fibre	2g
Sugar	3.4g

1— Cover the tofu with some kitchen paper, and then press it down with a heavy object for 15 minutes to get rid of the excess water.

2— Cut the tofu into 1cm (½ inch) cubes.

3— In a bowl, whisk together all the remaining ingredients for the tofu with just 1 tsp of the oil. Add in the tofu and toss lightly, coating the pieces well.

4— If you have time, marinate the tofu in the fridge for a minimum of 1 hour.

5— Heat a griddle pan over a medium heat. Pour in the remaining oil and, once hot, add the marinated tofu.

6— Once the tofu is crispy on one side (around 3–4 minutes cooking time), flip over to cook the other sides for a further few minute until golden and crispy.

7— Meanwhile, prepare your salad. Put the salad leaves into a large bowl and add the onion and tomatoes. Pour in the lemon juice and mix well.

8— Top the salad with cooked tofu.

Roasted chickpea salad ⓥ

PREP TIME	15 mins
COOK TIME	25 mins
SERVES	4

2 x 400g (14oz) cans of chickpeas,
   rinsed and drained
2 tbsp olive oil
3 tsp sumac
2 tsp smoked paprika
1 tsp salt
6 large garlic cloves, unpeeled
4 tbsp extra-virgin olive oil
4 tbsp lemon juice
300g cherry tomatoes, halved
1 cucumber, coarsely chopped
5 spring onions, finely chopped
15g (½oz) fresh parsley leaves
handful of pomegranate seeds
pepper

1— Position a rack in the centre of the oven and preheat the oven to 200°C (400°F), Gas Mark 6. Line a large baking sheet with parchment paper.

2— Toss the chickpeas with the olive oil, 1 tsp of the sumac, the paprika and a pinch of the salt. Season with pepper.

3— Wrap the garlic cloves in a small sheet of foil and place on the same baking sheet. Roast, stirring the chickpeas halfway through the cooking time, for 25–30 minutes or until crisp and golden brown. Allow to cool.

4— Unwrap the roasted garlic and squeeze the flesh into a serving bowl, discarding the skins. Mash the garlic using a fork. Stir in the extra-virgin olive oil, lemon juice, remaining 2 tsp of sumac and the remaining salt.

5— Add the tomatoes, cucumber, spring onion and parsley and toss to coat. Sprinkle with the chickpeas and pomegranate.

NUTRITIONAL INFORMATION

Calories	419kcal
Carbohydrates	40g
Protein	11.4g
Fat	25.5g
Fibre	11.1g
Sugar	11.7g

Coleslaw + Ⓥ

PREP TIME	10 mins
SERVES	6

500g (1lb 2oz) white cabbage,
    finely sliced
500g (1lb 2oz) red cabbage,
    finely sliced
4 large carrots, peeled and grated
4 spring onions, finely sliced
100g (3½oz) mixed seeds
    (I use pumpkin and sunflower
    seeds) (optional)

DRESSING
2 tbsp mayonnaise
    (regular or vegan)
4 tbsp apple cider vinegar, white
    wine vinegar or lemon juice
4 tsp Dijon mustard
8 tbsp olive oil
salt and pepper

1— Prepare all the vegetables and place in a large bowl. Mix in the seeds.

2— Place all the dressing ingredients in a small bowl or jar and whisk together.

3— Pour the dressing over the vegetables and seeds and mix together thoroughly.

NUTRITIONAL INFORMATION

Calories	352kcal
Carbohydrates	20.3g
Protein	6.9g
Fat	31.1g
Fibre	5.8g
Sugar	8.8g

Smashed potato salad + ⓥ

PREP TIME	10 mins
COOK TIME	50 mins
SERVES	6

1kg (2lb 4oz) baby potatoes
4 tbsp olive oil
1 tsp minced peeled fresh ginger
60g (2¼oz) Greek yogurt
    (or substitute with a
    dairy-free yogurt)
2 tbsp mayonnaise
    (regular or vegan)
1 tsp brown sugar
2 tsp chopped fresh thyme
2 tsp chopped fresh oregano
bunch of watercress, chopped
4 spring onions, thinly sliced
salt and pepper

1— Preheat the oven to 220°C (425°F), Gas Mark 7.

2— Put the potatoes in a large pan. Fill the pan with water until the potatoes are covered by 2.5cm (1 inch) of water. Season with salt and bring to a boil. Reduce the heat and simmer for 20–25 minutes until tender. Drain and return to the pot to dry.

3— Working with one potato at a time, place each under a glass and press to flatten.

4— Divide the oil between two baking sheets. Transfer the smashed potatoes to the baking sheets and turn to coat in the oil, then season with salt, pepper and the ginger. Roast, flipping once, for 20–25 minutes until golden. Remove from the oven and set aside to cool slightly.

5— Meanwhile, whisk together the yogurt, mayonnaise, brown sugar, thyme and oregano and season with salt and pepper.

6— Fold the warm potatoes into the dressing along with the watercress and spring onions. Season with salt and pepper.

NUTRITIONAL INFORMATION

Calories	252kcal
Carbohydrates	30.5g
Protein	3.5g
Fat	13.5g
Fibre	2g
Sugar	3.7g

Mushroom shawarma Buddha bowl ⓥ

PREP TIME	40 mins
MARINATING TIME	30 minutes
COOK TIME	20 mins
SERVES	2

MUSHROOM SHAWARMA
300g (10½oz) oyster or portobello
    mushrooms, trimmed and halved
1 tsp allspice
1 tsp ground cumin
1 tsp sumac
1 tsp ground coriander
1 tsp ground turmeric
1 tsp salt
1 tsp pepper
1 tbsp olive oil
2 garlic cloves, crushed

TZATZIKI
250g (9oz) coconut yogurt or other
    vegan yogurt (if not vegan,
    Greek yogurt works well)
½ cucumber, grated
1 garlic clove, crushed
2 tbsp lemon juice
½ tbsp fresh mint leaves, chopped
¼ tsp paprika
salt and pepper

SALAD
½ iceberg lettuce, chopped
2 large tomatoes, sliced
¼ red cabbage, sliced
½ cucumber,
    peeled into long strips
    using a swivel-head peeler
whole or sliced pickled chillies and
    sliced red onions (optional)

TO SERVE
2 pitta breads,
    toasted and cut into quarters

1— In a large bowl, mix the mushrooms with all the spices, salt and pepper, oil and garlic. Cover and allow to marinate for at least 30 minutes.

2— To make the tzatziki, mix all the ingredients together in a bowl and set aside to chill in the refrigerator.

3— Preheat the oven to 220°C (425°F), Gas Mark 7 and line a baking tray with parchment paper.

4— Spread the marinated mushrooms evenly on the prepared baking tray and roast for 20 minutes, turning halfway.

5— Assemble salad in a bowl – use the lettuce as a base and top with the remaining salad ingredients and mushrooms, arranging them in sections like a Buddha bowl.

6— Serve with a dollop of the tzatziki and the pitta bread tucked into the side.

NUTRITIONAL INFORMATION

Calories	201kcal
Carbohydrates	24.8g
Protein	7.1g
Fat	10.1g
Fibre	5.5g
Sugar	13.1g

NOTE: Excluding the pitta bread

Indian-spiced carrot salad ⓥ

PREP TIME	10 mins
COOK TIME	5 mins
SERVES	4

30g (1oz) sultanas
70g (2½oz) cashews
5 carrots,
    peeled and coarsely grated

DRESSING
2 tsp cumin seeds
juice of 1 lemon
2 tbsp olive oil
½ tsp salt
25g (1oz) fresh coriander,
    roughly chopped

1— Put the sultanas in a small bowl and cover with boiling water. Soak for 10 minutes or until nicely plumped, then drain and pat dry on kitchen paper.

2— Meanwhile, toast the cumin seeds in a dry frying pan for 1–2 minutes until golden. Tip the seeds into a small bowl and, using the same pan, add the cashew nuts and toast for 3 minutes until golden, then roughly chop.

3— Mix the remaining dressing ingredients with the toasted cumin seeds.

4— Add the grated carrots, sultanas and cashews to a serving bowl. Pour the dressing over, mix well and serve.

NUTRITIONAL INFORMATION

Calories	211kcal
Carbohydrates	19.6g
Protein	3.9g
Fat	18.5g
Fibre	3.2g
Sugar	9.3g

Lentil and
feta salad + ⓥ

PREP TIME	5 mins
SERVES	4

400g (14oz) can of green lentils,
    rinsed and drained
1 cucumber, finely diced
1 red pepper, finely diced
1 small red onion, finely diced
30g (1oz) fresh parsley,
    finely chopped
10g (¼oz) fresh mint leaves
75g (2½oz) feta cheese, crumbled
    (if vegan, replace with vegan
    feta cheese)
Balsamic dressing (see page 62)

1— Thoroughly combine all the salad ingredients together in a large bowl.

2— Once ready to serve, mix the dressing through the salad.

NUTRITIONAL INFORMATION

Calories	157kcal
Carbohydrates	21g
Protein	9.9g
Fat	4.7g
Fibre	5.1g
Sugar	5.7g

Dried fruit

USES

To flavour and sweeten food, add dried fruit to couscous or bulgur and to Middle Eastern dishes and curries, or enjoy as a snack with cacao nibs and raw nuts.

Information is often conflicting about dried fruit. It may be packed with nutrients, but it is also has much more sugar that fresh fruit weight for weight as almost all the water content has been removed. It can, however, be very useful to flavour and sweeten food naturally rather than using sugar or honey. Just be careful with portion sizes. For example, it's a good idea to mix a little dried fruit with a few nuts for an afternoon or mid-morning snack.

Despite being high on the glycaemic index, dried fruit in small quantities is beneficial as it contains all the nutrients of the original fruit – a 30g (1oz) portion of dried fruit counts as one of your five-a-day. It is generally a rich source of fibre and polyphenol antioxidants, which are associated with benefits such as better blood flow and digestive health, decreased oxidative damage and the reduced risk of many diseases.

Prunes are especially rich in fibre, potassium and vitamins K and A (beta carotene). Their high fibre and sorbitol content also makes them an effective natural laxative. Dates, however, have the highest antioxidant content of all dried fruit.

Always avoid dried fruit with added sugar. It is also worth checking the label for added sulphites; while these make the fruit look more appealing some people are sensitive to sulphites, which can lead to gut symptoms. Choose natural if you can – they will taste better!

Harissa aubergine steaks with giant couscous ⓥ

PREP TIME	15 mins
COOK TIME	30 mins
SERVES	4

2 aubergines
150g (5½oz) giant couscous
25g (1oz) fresh coriander,
  roughly chopped
25g (1oz) fresh parsley,
  roughly chopped

HARISSA GLAZE
2½ tbsp olive oil
4 tbsp harissa paste
1 tbsp maple syrup
  (or honey if not vegan)
2 tsp lemon juice
2 tbsp boiled water

TOPPINGS (OPTIONAL)
handful of pomegranate seeds
fresh mint leaves
walnuts

NUTRITIONAL INFORMATION

Calories	241kcal
Carbohydrates	27.3g
Protein	4.8g
Fat	14g
Fibre	9.6g
Sugar	11.7g

NOTE: Excluding the toppings

1— Preheat the oven to 220°C (425°F), Gas Mark 7 and line a baking tray with parchment paper.

2— Cut the aubergines in half lengthways and score the flesh quite deeply in a criss-cross pattern. Drizzle 2 tbsp of the olive oil over the cut surface of aubergine and rub in with your fingers. Place on the baking tray, cut-side down, and bake for 20 minutes.

3— To make the harissa glaze, combine all the ingredients.

4— Remove the tray from the oven, turn the aubergines over and spread over the harissa mix to coat the cut sides. Return to the oven for a further 10 minutes.

5— Meanwhile, bring a saucepan of salted water to the boil. Heat the remaining olive oil in a frying pan over a medium–high heat. Add the couscous to the frying pan and toast for 2 minutes until golden brown, then tip into the pan of boiling water and cook for 8–10 minutes until tender. Drain well.

6— Mix the couscous with the chopped coriander and parsley.

7— Serve the aubergines with the couscous and a scattering of pomegranate, mint leaves and walnuts.

Sweet potato falafel salad

PREP TIME	20 mins
COOK TIME	50 mins
SERVES	4

FALAFELS

1 large sweet potato
400g (14oz) can of chickpeas,
    rinsed and drained
4 garlic cloves, crushed
handful of fresh coriander leaves
2 heaped tsp ground coriander
1 heaped tsp ground cumin
2 tbsp olive oil
1 tsp sea salt
2 tbsp gram (chickpea) flour
    (or plain flour)

SALAD

1 small cauliflower
200g (7oz) giant couscous
2 small romaine lettuces, chopped
150g (5½oz) kale, chopped
1 avocado, sliced
handful of mixed seeds
150g (5½oz) cherry tomatoes, halved
1 cucumber, peeled into thin strips
    using a swivel-head peeler
½ red onion, thinly sliced
handful of your choice of fresh herbs
Balsamic dressing (see page 62)

NUTRITIONAL INFORMATION

Calories	637kcal
Carbohydrates	64.2g
Protein	17.9g
Fat	35.8g
Fibre	17.6g
Sugar	14.3g

1— Pierce the sweet potato a few times with a fork, then microwave for 10 minutes or until soft.

2— While the sweet potato is cooking, put the rest of the falafel ingredients, apart from the gram flour, into a blender or food processor. Blend until most of the mixture is broken down. It doesn't need to be completely smooth.

3— If the oven is not already on, preheat it to 180°C (350°F), Gas Mark 4 and line a baking tray with parchment paper.

4— Once the sweet potato has cooked, let it cool and peel off the skin.

5— Add the gram flour and sweet potato to the blended mixture and mix in with a spoon. The mixture should be easy to roll into balls. If the mixture is too wet, slowly add some more gram flour.

6— Take a heaped teaspoon's worth of the mixture and roll into a small ball (this should be smaller than a golf ball). Repeat until you have used up all the mixture.

7— Place the falafels onto the lined baking tray and bake for 25–30 minutes.

8— While the falafels are baking, roast the cauliflower for 30 minutes, or until cooked through and cook the giant couscous according to the packet instructions.

9— Assemble your salad, drizzle over the dressing and mix together.

10— Top the salad with the falafels to serve.

Chapter 4

Winter warmers

This chapter is to help you get through those cold, wintery evenings with some super-easy and quick heart-warming recipes – think hearty soups, speedy ramen and flavourful curries. These dishes require minimum fuss and common pantry ingredients: complete nourishment and comfort in a bowl!

Peanut tofu noodles ⓥ

PREP TIME	25 mins
COOK TIME	25 mins
SERVES	4

NOODLES
400g (14oz) extra-firm tofu,
    drained
225g (8oz) dried noodles
    of choice
2 tbsp cornflour
½ tsp salt
1½ tbsp olive oil
3 garlic cloves, finely chopped
1 carrot, julienned
½ broccoli, cut into small florets

PEANUT SAUCE
90g (3¼oz) peanut butter
3 tbsp soy sauce or tamari
4 tsp rice vinegar
20g (¾oz) maple or agave syrup
    (or honey if not vegan)
2 tsp sesame oil

TOPPINGS
handful of chopped peanuts
1 tsp black sesame seeds

1— Cover the tofu with some kitchen paper, and then press it down with a heavy object for 15 minutes to get rid of the excess water. Cut into 1½cm (1 inch) cubes.

2— Heat a pan of water and cook the noodles according to the packet instructions. Drain and rinse under cold water after cooking.

3— Meanwhile, make the peanut sauce by combining all the ingredients.

4— In a separate bowl, toss together the tofu, cornflour and salt until the tofu is well coated.

5— Heat 1 tbsp of the olive oil in a non-stick frying pan over a medium–high heat. Add the tofu in a single layer and cook for 3–4 minutes on all sides, until most sides are golden brown. Set aside.

6— Add the remaining ½ tbsp of oil to the pan and sauté the garlic for 1–2 minutes before adding the carrot and broccoli. Cook for 3–4 minutes until the veggies have softened, stirring frequently.

7— Add the peanut sauce along with the cooked noodles and tofu. Toss until everything is well combined. Give it a taste and add more soy sauce, if needed.

8— Top with the chopped peanuts and black sesame seeds.

NUTRITIONAL INFORMATION

Calories	456kcal
Carbohydrates	42g
Protein	26.1g
Fat	24.4g
Fibre	8.7g
Sugar	7.8g

Thai-inspired cauliflower soup ⓥ

PREP TIME	10 mins
COOK TIME	30 mins
SERVES	6

1 large head of cauliflower, roughly
    chopped, leaves reserved
3 tbsp olive oil
1 tsp sea salt
1 onion, chopped
4 large carrots, chopped
2 tbsp chopped peeled fresh ginger
3 garlic cloves, minced
1 tsp ground turmeric
4 tbsp yellow Thai curry paste
    (can substitute with red)
1⅛ litres (2 pints) vegetable stock
400ml (14fl oz) can of coconut milk
sea salt and pepper

TOPPINGS
spring onions, sliced
fresh coriander
fresh chilli
freshly squeezed lime juice

1— Preheat the oven to 200°C (400°F), Gas Mark 6. Line a baking sheet with parchment paper.

2— Put the chopped cauliflower on the baking sheet, drizzle with 1 tbsp of the olive oil and sprinkle with the salt. Roast the cauliflower for 30 minutes, or until it is soft and golden. In the last 5 minutes of roasting, add the cauliflower leaves.

3— While the cauliflower is roasting, begin the soup. Heat the remaining olive oil in a large pan over medium–high heat. Add the onion and sauté for 5 minutes. Add the carrot and continue to cook, stirring occasionally, for about 10 minutes until both the carrot and onion are brown.

4— Add the ginger and garlic and cook for 1 minute. Add the turmeric and Thai curry paste and cook for 1 more minute.

5— Add the stock and bring the soup to the boil. Once boiling, reduce the heat and simmer for a further 10 minutes.

6— Once the cauliflower is roasted, add it to the pan, reserving a few small pieces, along with their leaves, for garnish.

7— Using a stick blender (or, working in small batches, using a regular blender) blend the soup until it is very smooth. Add the coconut milk and season to taste with sea salt and pepper.

8— Serve the soup garnished with the reserved cauliflower florets and any, or all, of the other garnishes.

NUTRITIONAL INFORMATION

Calories	123cal
Carbohydrates	7.3g
Protein	2.2g
Fat	10.2g
Fibre	1.8g
Sugar	2.9g

Sweet potato kitchari

PREP TIME	15 mins
COOK TIME	45 mins
SERVES	4

200g (7oz) yellow mung dal
220g (7½oz) basmati rice
    (you can use brown rice but
    soak overnight and allow
    longer cooking time)
2 tbsp olive oil or butter or ghee
2 tsp ground turmeric
2 tsp mustard seeds
2 tsp minced peeled fresh ginger
1 tsp ground coriander
1 tsp ground cumin
1⅛ litres (2 pints) water
1 large sweet potato,
    peeled and cubed (can
    substitute with 400g (14oz) of
    any squash or root vegetable)
salt and pepper

1— Rinse the mung dal and rice until the water runs clear.

2— Heat the oil or butter in a large pan. Add all of the spices and sauté together over a medium heat for 1 minute until fragrant.

3— Stir in the mung dal and rice. Add the water, along with the sweet potato. Bring to the boil, then reduce to a simmer, lid on.

4— Cook for at least 40 minutes or until the dal and rice are completely soft (easily squashed between finger and thumb) and stir through to mash the sweet potato.

5— Season with salt and pepper, to taste.

NUTRITIONAL INFORMATION

Calories	333kcal
Carbohydrates	58.3g
Protein	5.7g
Fat	8.4g
Fibre	3.4g
Sugar	2.8g

Note— Kitchari is a traditional ayurvedic recipe, that's nourishing and easy to digest. Leftover kitchari can be refrigerated in an airtight container for 3 days. Reheat on the hob, adding water as needed to reach the desired consistency.

Veggie minestrone Ⓥ

PREP TIME	10 mins
COOK TIME	35 mins
SERVES	4

1 tbsp olive oil
1 onion, finely sliced
3–4 garlic cloves, crushed
2 celery sticks, diced
3 carrots, diced
120g (4oz) small pasta shapes
1.5 litres (2½ pints)
    vegetable stock
1 broccoli, cut into small florets
large handful of spinach leaves
salt and pepper
crusty bread, to serve

1— Heat the olive oil in a large saucepan, add the onion and fry over a low–medium heat for 5 minutes, stirring occasionally. Add the garlic, celery and carrot, then fry, stirring occasionally, for another 7–10 minutes.

2— Add the pasta and stock, then simmer for 15 minutes. Stir in the broccoli florets and spinach, then simmer for 4–5 minutes more. Add in salt and pepper to taste and serve with some crusty bread.

NUTRITIONAL INFORMATION

Calories	203kcal
Carbohydrates	35.2g
Protein	6.5g
Fat	4.6g
Fibre	3.6g
Sugar	6.5g

NOTE: Excluding the bread

Pulses

USES

Soak overnight and freeze in batches ready to cook from fresh. Add to soups and meat and veggie stews. Lentils are especially good for thickening soups instead of potatoes. All pulses lend themselves greatly to heat and spices, so they make wonderful curries.

Generally, all pulses are all a great source of fibre, protein and thiamine (B1), folate, iron, magnesium, copper and manganese.

The high protein content of beans means they are a great replacement for meat, fish and eggs. Together with fibre, protein helps slow the transition of glucose into the bloodstream. This will help level out the peaks and troughs, which cause cravings and energy highs and lows, often termed the 'blood-sugar roller coaster'. Ensuring a meal has both protein and fibre will help stabilize this and assist us in making better food choices. This is especially useful for individuals with blood-sugar imbalances, such as diabetes and hypoglycaemia. It should be noted however that beans are a source of incomplete protein, so ideally they need to be eaten accompanied by another grain or pulse to provide the complete complement of amino acids (the building blocks for protein). This is important for vegan diets.

Pulses are also incredibly heart healthy. Their high soluble fibre content may help lower cholesterol due to its ability to bind to bile acids, which prevent the cholesterol from being re-absorbed into the body. An increase in bile acid production decreases the pool of cholesterol in the liver, which in turn will decrease circulating cholesterol in the blood. Specific phytochemicals in plant cell membranes, called phytosterols, are also believed to have further cholesterol-removing effects. A double whammy!

Lentils are high in prebiotic fibre, which is the type of fibre that 'feeds' good bacteria, helping them flourish in our gut microflora. A diet high in fibre has numerous health benefits, including a lower risk of developing bowel cancer. Many people, however, find they are sensitive to pulses as they undergo fast cooking processes when canned. If this is the case, soaking dried pulses overnight and cooking until very tender is always a better option. Also, eating a single variety at a time can help you discover which ones your body can tolerate, and which ones to avoid.

Jackfruit curry ⓥ

PREP TIME	10 mins
COOK TIME	1 hour
SERVES	6

1 tbsp coconut oil
1 tsp cumin seeds
1 tsp mustard seeds
1–2 green chillies, chopped
    (depending on how hot
    you like your curry)
2 white onions, chopped
6 garlic cloves, chopped
2½cm (1 inch) piece of fresh ginger,
    peeled and grated
1½ tsp ground coriander
1 tsp ground cumin
1 tsp ground turmeric
2 tbsp tomato purée
2 x 400g (14oz) cans of green
    jackfruit pieces, rinsed and
    drained, roughly chopped
400g (14oz) can of chopped tomatoes
3 tbsp coconut cream,
    plus extra to drizzle

TO SERVE
Courgette raita (see page 129)
steamed rice

1— Pour the oil into a large saucepan over a medium heat. Add the cumin and mustard seeds and cook for 1 minute, then add the chopped chilli, onion, garlic and ginger. Cook until the onion is soft and translucent.

2— Add the ground coriander, cumin, turmeric, tomato purée and jackfruit. Mix together, pour in the chopped tomatoes, cover the pan and cook for 40–45 minutes or until the jackfruit is soft. If the sauce is too thick, you can gradually add in some water.

3— Add the coconut cream and mix everything together. Gently cook, uncovered, until the sauce has thickened.

4— Serve the curry with a little coconut cream drizzled over and the raita and rice.

NUTRITIONAL INFORMATION

Calories	162kcal
Carbohydrates	32.7g
Protein	3.1g
Fat	3.9g
Fibre	2.5g
Sugar	23.5g

NOTE: Excluding the raita and rice

Rajma ⓥ

PREP TIME	5 mins
COOK TIME	20 mins
SERVES	2

1 tbsp vegetable oil
1 tbsp cumin seeds
1 onion, finely chopped
3 garlic cloves, minced
thumb-sized piece of fresh ginger,
    peeled and grated
1 tsp ground coriander
1 tsp ground cumin
1 tsp ground turmeric
2 tsp garam masala
400g (14oz) can
    of chopped tomatoes
400g (14oz) can of kidney beans,
    rinsed and drained
salt and pepper

1— Heat the oil in a large pan over a medium heat and fry the cumin seeds for 1 minute.

2— Add the onion and allow to soften. Add the garlic and ginger and cook for a further minute.

3— Add the ground coriander, cumin, turmeric, and garam masala.

4— Add the chopped tomatoes and kidney beans. Half-fill one of the cans with water and pour it into the mixture. Season with salt and pepper to taste.

5— Cover with a lid and simmer for 15 minutes to cook and thicken the rajma.

NUTRITIONAL INFORMATION

Calories	278kcal
Carbohydrates	39g
Protein	13g
Fat	8.4g
Fibre	8.8g
Sugar	13.2g

Note—This dish originated in north India and is a recipe for when you have nothing in the fridge but you're in need of something warming, nourishing and cheap. Just a 90g (3¼oz) serving of cooked kidney beans provides you with 7g of fibre and 8g of protein, making them a great option to boost your protein and fibre intake without a lot of calories. They are also cheap to buy, so they're definitely one to keep in your pantry.

Crispy gnocchi traybake + Ⓥ

PREP TIME	5 mins
COOK TIME	40 mins
SERVES	4

500g (1lb 2oz) gnocchi,
   fresh or frozen (no need
   to defrost)
1 large red pepper,
   deseeded and chopped
150g (5½oz) cherry tomatoes
1 courgette,
   sliced into half-moons
1 large red onion, chopped
4 garlic cloves,
   whole and crushed with
   the flat of the knife blade
4 sprigs of fresh rosemary
1 tsp chilli flakes
1 tsp sea salt
1 tsp pepper
3 tbsp olive oil
100g (3½oz) feta (or vegan feta),
   crumbled
handful of fresh basil leaves

1— Position a rack in the middle of the oven and preheat to 200°C (400°F), Gas Mark 6. Line a rimmed baking sheet with parchment paper.

2— Put the gnocchi, red pepper, tomatoes, courgette, onion, garlic, rosemary, chilli flakes, salt and pepper in a large bowl. Drizzle with the oil and gently toss to combine. Spread out the mixture evenly in a single layer on the baking sheet.

3— Roast, stirring halfway through, until the gnocchi are plump and the vegetables are tender, about 30–40 minutes.

4— Top with the crumbled feta and basil leaves to serve.

NUTRITIONAL INFORMATION

Calories	267kcal
Carbohydrates	34.1g
Protein	6.5g
Fat	11g
Fibre	2.4g
Sugar	4.2g

Chilli with baked sweet potatoes ⓥ

PREP TIME	10 mins
COOK TIME	1 hour
SERVES	6

6 sweet potatoes
1 tbsp olive oil
1 white onion, chopped
1 red pepper, deseeded and diced
1 green pepper, deseeded and diced
4 garlic cloves, crushed
1–2 tsp chilli powder
1 tbsp dried oregano
2 tsp ground cumin
400g (14oz) can of kidney beans,
   rinsed and drained
400g (14oz) can of black beans,
   rinsed and drained
400g (14oz) can
   of chopped tomatoes
350ml (12fl oz) vegetable stock
½ tsp pepper
½ tsp salt

TO SERVE
salad leaves
avocado

NUTRITIONAL INFORMATION

Calories	246kcal
Carbohydrates	52g
Protein	9.7g
Fat	1g
Fibre	12g
Sugar	11g

NOTE: Excluding the avocado

1— Preheat the oven to 200°C (400°F), Gas Mark 6 and line a baking sheet with parchment paper.

2— Scrub the sweet potatoes to clean then use a fork to poke holes into the top of each one. Place on the baking sheet and bake for 50 minutes–1 hour.

3— Meanwhile, heat the oil in a large saucepan over a medium heat. Add the onion and peppers and cook for 8–10 minutes, stirring occasionally until soft, then add in the garlic and cook for a further minute.

4— Add the chilli powder, oregano and cumin. Stir to combine and cook for a couple more minutes. If the pan starts to dry out, add a splash of water.

5— Add the rest of the ingredients and simmer gently for 15–20 minutes.

6— If you want your chilli to have less texture and more thickness, use a stick blender in the pan to pulse the chilli a few times to blend just a bit of it. Alternatively, add a big scoop to a blender, pulse a few times then pour back into the pan.

7— Turn off the heat and let the chilli sit for 5 minutes to thicken a little.

8— Serve with the baked sweet potatoes, salad leaves and avocado.

Note — You can swap the beans for any beans you have – chickpeas, black-eyed beans, white beans or pinto beans all work well.

Sweetcorn chowder ●ᵥ

PREP TIME	10 mins
COOK TIME	25 mins
SERVES	4

1–2 tbsp olive oil
2 large leeks,
    thinly sliced into rings
2 celery sticks, diced
4 garlic cloves, chopped
400g (14oz) frozen sweetcorn
    (or use canned, rinsed
    and drained)
320g (11½oz) baby potatoes
    (about 12–13), thinly sliced
850ml (1½ pints) vegetable stock
    (2 veggie stock cubes in
    boiling hot water)
1 tsp paprika
½ tsp ground turmeric
1 tsp salt
½ tsp pepper
400ml (14fl oz) can
    of coconut milk

TOPPINGS (OPTIONAL)
spring onions, sliced
coriander
lime wedges

1— Heat the oil in a large pan over a medium heat. Add the leeks and sauté for 4–5 minutes, stirring until they just begin to get tender.

2— Add the celery and garlic, lower the heat to medium–low and sauté until the leeks are tender – about 5–6 minutes.

3— Add the sweetcorn, potato, stock, paprika, turmeric, salt and pepper and bring to a simmer.

4— Cover, turn the heat to medium–low and let it simmer for about 10–12 minutes until the potatoes are tender.

5— Ladle half the soup into a blender and whizz until smooth. Pour the smooth half back into the unblended soup and mix to combine.

6— Taste and add extra seasoning, if needed.

7— Scatter over some spring onion, coriander and serve with a wedge of lime.

NUTRITIONAL INFORMATION

Calories	260kcal
Carbohydrates	36.5g
Protein	4.6g
Fat	10.9g
Fibre	5.5g
Sugar	4.9g

Vegetable biriyani ⓥ

PREP TIME	10 mins
COOK TIME	45 mins
SERVES	6

3 tbsp olive oil
2 white onions, finely chopped
3 garlic cloves, crushed
1 tbsp minced peeled fresh ginger
2 tbsp tomato purée
120ml (4fl oz) water
100g (3½oz) peas
1 carrot, sliced into 1cm
   (½ inch) discs
2 floury potatoes,
   peeled and chopped
1 green pepper,
   deseeded and sliced
½ cauliflower,
   chopped into small florets
2 tsp salt
½ tsp pepper
1 tsp chilli powder
2 tsp garam masala
½ tsp ground turmeric
1 tsp ground cumin
1 tsp ground coriander
½ tsp cinnamon
950ml (1½ pints) vegetable stock
   (2 veggie stock cubes in
   boiling hot water)
370g (13oz) basmati rice,
   well rinsed and drained
handful of roughly chopped
   fresh coriander (optional)

1— Pour the olive oil into a large pan over a medium–high heat.

2— Add the onion and cook until translucent, about 3–4 minutes.

3— Stir in the garlic, ginger, tomato purée and water. Bring to a simmer and cook until the water has evaporated, about 10 minutes.

4— Add in the peas, carrot, potato, green pepper and cauliflower and stir well.

5— Stir in the salt, pepper, chilli powder, garam masala, turmeric, cumin, coriander and cinnamon.

6— Pour in the vegetable stock and bring to the boil.

7— Add the rice to the pan, reduce the heat to low and cook, covered, for 20–25 minutes.

8— Turn off the heat and let sit, covered, for 5 minutes before serving, garnished with some coriander, if using.

NUTRITIONAL INFORMATION

Calories	290kcal
Carbohydrates	52.9g
Protein	6.1g
Fat	6.2g
Fibre	4.1g
Sugar	4.2g

Tofu ramen + Ⓥ

PREP TIME	45 mins
COOK TIME	20 mins
SERVES	2

200g (7oz) extra-firm tofu, drained

MARINADE
2 tbsp soy sauce
1 tsp cornflour
2 garlic cloves, crushed
2 tsp minced peeled fresh ginger

BROTH
2 tbsp sesame oil
4cm (1½ inch) piece of fresh ginger,
    peeled and finely chopped
4 garlic cloves, finely chopped
1 red chilli, chopped
125g (4½oz) shiitake mushrooms,
    sliced
750ml (1¼ pints) vegetable stock
    (1 vegetable stock cube)
2 tbsp miso paste
120g (4oz) ramen noodles

TOPPINGS
3 spring onions, sliced
1 red chilli, sliced
1 tsp sesame seeds
1 boiled egg, sliced in half (optional)
handful of pea shoots

1— Cover the tofu with some kitchen paper, and then press it down with a heavy object for 15 minutes to get rid of the excess water. Cut into bite-sized cubes.

2— Mix all the marinade ingredients together and allow the tofu to marinate for around 20 minutes.

3— Add 1 tbsp of the sesame oil to a pan over medium heat. Fry the ginger, garlic and chilli for 2 minutes, stirring to ensure they don't burn.

4— Add the shiitake mushrooms and cook for about 3–4 minutes.

5— Add the vegetable stock and whisk in the miso paste until dissolved. Leave to simmer for 10 minutes, uncovered.

6— Pour the remaining sesame oil into a frying pan over a medium–high heat and fry the tofu for a few minutes on each side until golden.

7— Add the noodles to the broth for the final 5 minutes of cooking, then serve in bowls with the fried tofu.

8— Garnish with the spring onion, chilli, sesame seeds, boiled egg and pea shoots.

NUTRITIONAL INFORMATION

Calories	229kcal
Carbohydrates	29.3g
Protein	10.7g
Fat	8.3g
Fibre	2.4g
Sugar	3.4g

NOTE: Excluding the toppings

Ginger

Ginger can be used fresh, dried or as an oil or juice. Simply steep the sliced root and infuse to make a refreshing tea or boil with turmeric root to make a stronger concoction. The root can be grated fresh into green juices, salad dressings, soups and curries. Use the dried powder for wholegrain muffins, oat cookies and granola.

Closely related to turmeric and galangal, ginger is an incredibly healing spice and has been used as a natural remedy for thousands of years. The unique flavour and fragrance come from its natural oils, in particular, 6-gingerol, the main bioactive compound responsible for ginger's medicinal properties. Ginger's anti-nausea effects are well known – the root can be especially useful for cases of morning sickness during pregnancy.

Gingerol can also benefit glucose control, which can protect against the development of type 2 diabetes. It's also been thought to help with weight loss and even protect against stomach ulcers by speeding up the process of digestion.

Ginger's healing and anti-inflammatory properties are thanks to certain compounds which work on the same biological pathways as some painkillers such as ibuprofen. This explains its success in easing menstrual pains and relieving joint and muscle pain. This humble root's super antioxidant and anti-inflammatory properties are also vital in strengthening the body's defences against diseases and improving metabolic health. There is also some evidence that fresh ginger has potential antiviral effects, so including ginger in your diet where possible can be incredibly beneficial.

Aubergine and chickpea bake + ⓥ

PREP TIME	10 mins
COOK TIME	35 mins
SERVES	4

2 aubergines, cut lengthways
     into 5mm (¼ inch) slices
3 tbsp olive oil
2 onions, finely chopped
3 garlic cloves, crushed
1 red pepper,
     deseeded and chopped
400g (14oz) can of chickpeas
3 tbsp harissa paste
400g (14oz) can
     of chopped tomatoes
125g (4½oz) ball of mozzarella,
     torn (if vegan, replace with
     vegan feta cheese)
handful of fresh parsley
salt and pepper

1— Preheat the oven to 200°C (400°F), Gas Mark 6.

2— Brush both sides of the aubergine slices with 2 tbsp of the oil, lay on baking sheets, season and bake for 15–20 minutes until tender, turning halfway through.

3— While the aubergines are roasting, make the chickpeas. Heat the remaining oil in a large frying pan. Tip in the onion and garlic and cook until the onion has softened. Add in the chopped red pepper. Cook for 5–7 minutes until the pepper has softened.

4— Stir though the chickpeas, harissa paste and the chopped tomatoes, plus ½ can of water. Simmer for 10–15 minutes until the sauce has thickened.

5— Spoon a layer of sauce into a small baking dish. Top with aubergine slices and repeat, finishing with a layer of aubergine. Scatter with mozzarella and bake for a further 15 minutes until the cheese is golden and bubbling. If using feta cheese, it will need less cooking time – around 10 minutes.

6— Top with fresh parsley and serve.

NUTRITIONAL INFORMATION

Calories	185kcal
Carbohydrates	16.5g
Protein	6.9g
Fat	11.3g
Fibre	5.7g
Sugar	5.9g

Veggie patties ⓥ

PREP TIME	10 mins
COOK TIME	1½ hours
SERVES	5

2 sweet potatoes
400g (14oz) can of black beans,
    rinsed and drained
2 tsp extra virgin olive oil
1 small onion, finely chopped
1 tbsp paprika
1 tsp garam masala
1 tsp garlic powder
1 tsp sea salt
50g (1¾oz) fresh coriander,
    finely chopped

TO SERVE
juice of 1 lemon
mayonnaise (regular or vegan)
pitta (optional)

1— Preheat the oven to 200°C (400°F), Gas Mark 6 and line a baking sheet with parchment paper.

2— Scrub the sweet potatoes to clean then use a fork to poke holes into the top of each one. Place on the baking sheet and bake for 50 minutes–1 hour.

3— Put the beans and 1 tsp of the oil in a high-speed blender and pulse briefly.

4— Transfer the bean mixture to a large bowl, scoop out the flesh of the sweet potatoes and add with the onion, spices, garlic powder, salt and coriander. Use your hands to combine the ingredients well.

5— Reduce the oven temperature to 180°C (350°F), Gas Mark 4.

6— Divide the mixture into 10 portions and form into round kebab patties.

7— Place on the baking sheet and bake for 25–30 minutes or until golden brown.

8— Serve hot with a squeeze of lemon juice and some spicy mayonnaise. You can enjoy 'as they are' or stuff them into pitta pockets with your favourite fillings, like some salad leaves, cucumbers and tomatoes.

NUTRITIONAL INFORMATION

Calories	120kcal
Carbohydrates	25.2g
Protein	4.8g
Fat	3.6g
Fibre	6.8g
Sugar	4.1g

NOTE: Excluding the pitta

Chapter 5

Snacks & energy boosters

If you're looking for on-the-go snacks to help fuel your day, or something to graze on while you cosy up on the sofa, this chapter has got you covered. Loaded nachos, spicy pakoras and some crispy potato skins, these recipes will become staples in your household.

Corn ribs
with smoky mayo + ⓥ

PREP TIME	5 mins
COOK TIME	30 mins
SERVES	2

2 corn on the cob
½ tsp paprika
½ tsp garlic powder
½ tsp salt
¼ tsp pepper
1 tbsp olive oil
juice of ½ lemon
handful of fresh coriander,
   chopped

SMOKY MAYO
4 tbsp good-quality mayonnaise
   (regular or vegan)
juice of ½ lime
1 tsp sriracha (or more if you like
   super spicy!)
½ tsp paprika

1— Preheat the oven to 190°C (375°F), Gas Mark 5 and line a baking tray
   with parchment paper.

2— Cut your corn into quarters. Stand a cob vertically on the chopping
   board and, using a large sharp knife, very carefully cut through the
   centre of it. Then repeat using the same technique, cutting it in half
   again so you get quarters.

3— Combine the paprika, garlic powder, salt, pepper and oil in a bowl,
   then brush the seasoning over the corn ribs.

4— Lay the seasoned corn on the lined tray and bake for 25–30 minutes.

5— Meanwhile make the smoky mayo by mixing the ingredients together
   in a small bowl.

6— Once your ribs are ready, squeeze on some lemon juice, sprinkle over
   the chopped coriander and serve with the smoky mayo.

NUTRITIONAL INFORMATION

Calories	285kcal
Carbohydrates	21.7g
Protein	3.8g
Fat	22g
Fibre	2.5g
Sugar	4.8g

Crispy potato skin chips

PREP TIME	5 mins
COOK TIME	25 mins
SERVES	4

peelings from 6 large potatoes
1 tbsp olive oil
½ tsp salt
½ tsp pepper
1 tsp oregano

1— Preheat the oven to 200°C (400°F), Gas Mark 6.

2— Soak the peelings in cold water (this helps prevent them from discolouring while you continue to peel), then remove them and drain.

3— Dry the peelings on kitchen paper. The aim is to get as much of the moisture removed as possible before baking them.

4— Add the peelings to a large bowl with the oil, salt, pepper and oregano. Mix well.

5— Spread the peelings evenly onto a lined baking sheet.

6— Bake in the oven for 20–25 minutes, turning the potato skins halfway.

NUTRITIONAL INFORMATION

Calories	28kcal
Carbohydrates	5.1g
Protein	0.6g
Fat	0.5g
Fibre	0.6g
Sugar	0.2g

Courgette raita + ⓥ

PREP TIME	30 mins
COOK TIME	10 mins
DRAINING TIME	20 mins
SERVES	4

2 medium courgettes
½ tsp salt
350g (12oz) Greek yogurt
   (or your choice of non-dairy
   yogurt – coconut yogurt
   works well)
1 tbsp olive oil
½ tsp cumin seeds
½ tsp mustard seeds
1 white onion, finely sliced
   into half-moon slices
salt and pepper

1— Grate the courgettes coarsely, sprinkle with the salt and let it drain in a colander for 20 minutes.

2— Beat the yogurt with a fork in a bowl until creamy and smooth.

3— Heat the oil in a frying pan and add the cumin and mustard seeds. When the mustard seeds pop, add the onion. Sauté the onion until translucent and tender.

4— While the onion is frying, squeeze as much liquid as possible out of the courgette using a clean tea towel. Add to the frying pan and, using a spatula, separate the courgette clumps. Cook for about 3 minutes.

5— Remove from the heat and allow to cool before stirring through the yogurt. Taste and add extra salt and pepper according to taste.

NUTRITIONAL INFORMATION

Calories	101kcal
Carbohydrates	8.5g
Protein	4.5g
Fat	5.5g
Fibre	0.9g
Sugar	7.3g

Sweet potato chaat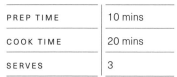

PREP TIME	10 mins
COOK TIME	20 mins
SERVES	3

2 large sweet potatoes,
    peeled and diced into 2½cm
    (1 inch) cubes
2 tbsp olive oil
½ tsp chaat masala,
    plus extra to sprinkle
½ tsp salt
50g (1¾oz) peanuts
1 small red onion, finely chopped
2 tsp tamarind chutney
large handful of fresh coriander,
    finely chopped
juice of 1 lime
drizzle of coconut yogurt
    (or your choice of yogurt)
handful of pomegranate seeds
    (optional)

1— Preheat the oven to 220°C (425°F), Gas Mark 7 and line a baking tray with parchment paper.

2— Add the sweet potato, olive oil, chaat masala and salt to a bowl and mix well until all the sweet potato cubes are covered with the oil and spices.

3— Spread out on the lined baking tray in a single layer. Roast for 15–20 minutes until the cubes are tender, yet still retain their shape.

4— Meanwhile place the peanuts into a frying pan over a medium heat. Toast for around 4–5 minutes, stirring often until lightly toasted.

5— Remove the sweet potato from the oven and let it cool slightly.

6— Once cooled, add to a large bowl along with the toasted peanuts, onion, tamarind chutney, coriander and lime juice. Mix well until all the potato cubes are coated.

7— Serve the sweet potato topped with a drizzle of yogurt, a sprinkle of chaat masala and the pomegranate seeds.

NUTRITIONAL INFORMATION

Calories	241 kcal
Carbohydrates	32g
Protein	6.6g
Fat	19.7g
Fibre	5.7g
Sugar	6.9g

Mixed nuts

USES
Nuts are great as a snack, paired with fruit, toasted and added to salads, grain dishes and sprinkled onto desserts.

Nuts are convenient, tasty and nutritious. Each type of nut has a different nutritional profile, but they do share some things in common. They are high in protective antioxidants that can help prevent cell damage and they are also high in the good type of fats that have proven health benefits. Studies suggest that nuts can aid weight management: research shows that the body doesn't absorb all the calories, as a portion of fat stays trapped within the nut's fibrous wall during digestion.

WALNUTS have a very impressive nutrient profile and great heart-health benefits as they are a good source of omega-3 fats, namely alpha-linolenic acid (ALA), more of which is found in walnuts than any other type of nut. ALA is essential for good health, but our bodies can't make it, so we need to get it from the foods we eat. ALA has been shown to reduce the risk of developing heart disease and to help reduce cholesterol levels. We can also get ALA from seeds and vegetable oils. These omega-3 fats coupled with walnuts' polyphenol (antioxidant) capacity, both of which are anti-inflammatory, means that incorporating these nuts into our diet may improve blood lipids and cholesterol and other cardiovascular risks.

ALMONDS confer similar benefits, with the added advantage of their skin providing a source of prebiotics for the gut, and they are also especially high in vitamin E. While other water-soluble antioxidants, such as vitamin C, flavonoids and polyphenols, perform their vital functions in the fluids of cells, vitamin E, by contrast, is a fat-soluble nutrient and protects the cell's membranes, as do the omega-3 fats in nuts. Healthy cell membranes are vital to health, not only for the transport of nutrients into cells but also for expelling toxins. Vitamin E also acts as an anti-ageing nutrient in the body and is important for skin and eye health.

PISTACHIOS are a good source of protein and the carotenoids lutein and zeaxanthin – both great for eye health. Pistachios are high in flavonoids, which have all the usual antioxidant and anti-inflammatory benefits, plus they balance cholesterol and triglyceride levels and help to lower blood pressure.

HAZELNUTS are good sources of vitamin E and copper and are very high in manganese, a lesser-known mineral that is essential for bone health, cognitive function and bile formation.

The king of nuts must be the BRAZIL NUT. High in vitamin E, magnesium and especially high in selenium – in fact, Brazil nuts are one of the best food sources available. Selenium prevents cell damage, it is an essential mineral for thyroid health as well as for glutathione production, a powerful antioxidant, which makes selenium vital for immune health, as well as protecting our body from DNA damage and all its associated diseases.

Korean tofu bites Ⓥ

PREP TIME	20 mins
COOK TIME	15 mins
SERVES	4

TOFU
280g (10oz) extra-firm tofu,
    drained
1 tbsp olive oil

SAUCE
3 tbsp ketchup
1½ tbsp gochujang paste
½ tbsp soy sauce or tamari
½ tbsp maple syrup
    (or honey if not vegan)
1 tsp sesame oil
2 garlic cloves, crushed

TOPPINGS
handful of sesame seeds
    (optional)
2 spring onions, finely chopped

1— Combine the sauce ingredients in a bowl. Mix them together well and set aside.

2— Cover the tofu with some kitchen paper, and then press it down with a heavy object for 15 minutes to get rid of the excess water. Cut into 1cm (½ inch) cubes.

3— Add the oil to a frying pan over a medium–high heat. Pan-fry the tofu for 2–3 minutes on all sides until golden brown.

4— Pour the sauce into the pan and gently coat the tofu. Cook for a few minutes.

5— Place in a serving bowl and sprinkle with sesame seeds, if using, and spring onions.

6— Enjoy as a snack or even serve with rice or noodles.

NUTRITIONAL INFORMATION

Calories	192kcal
Carbohydrates	11.1g
Protein	10.5g
Fat	12.3g
Fibre	2.2g
Sugar	6g

Crunchy halloumi chips + ⓥ

PREP TIME	10 mins
COOK TIME	25 mins
SERVES	8

2 x 250g (9oz) blocks of halloumi,
  cut into chips
50g (1¾oz) plain flour
50g (1¾oz) cornflakes, crushed
2 tsp paprika
3 tsp garlic powder
1 egg or 1 flaxseed egg, beaten

1— Preheat the oven to 190°C (375°F), Gas Mark 5 and line a baking tray with parchment paper.

2— Pat the cheese dry with a clean tea towel or kitchen paper.

3— Put the flour, crushed cornflakes, paprika and garlic powder onto a plate and mix well.

4— Put the beaten egg in a shallow bowl.

5— Coat the halloumi first in the beaten egg, then in the flour mixture and pop onto the prepared baking tray.

6— Bake for 20–25 minutes, turning halfway.

NUTRITIONAL INFORMATION

Calories	240kcal
Carbohydrates	11.1g
Protein	16.6g
Fat	14.8g
Fibre	0.4g
Sugar	1.9g

Note — Halloumi has a high salt content, so you can swap the halloumi for paneer. If you are dairy free, you can substitute with vegan halloumi.

Nachos 🅥

PREP TIME	15 mins
SERVES	4

150g (5½oz) walnuts
2 tbsp olive oil
1 tbsp tomato purée or ketchup
1 tbsp crushed garlic
1 tsp paprika
½ tsp cayenne pepper
1 tsp ground cumin
½ tsp salt
200g (7oz) tortilla chips

TOPPINGS (OPTIONAL)
2 large tomatoes, diced
1 ripe avocado,
    stone removed and diced
½ red onion, diced
25g (1oz) fresh coriander,
    roughly chopped
1 lime, sliced into wedges
jalapeño slices
soured cream

1— Put the walnuts, olive oil, tomato purée or ketchup, garlic, paprika, cayenne pepper, cumin and salt in a high-speed blender.

2— Gently pulse for 10–15 seconds. Do not over-pulse or it will become a purée – it should resemble minced taco meat. Taste and adjust the flavour as needed.

3— Arrange the tortilla chips on a large tray and spread a layer of the walnut taco mix over the top.

4— Sprinkle over your choice of toppings.

NUTRITIONAL INFORMATION

Calories	619kcal
Carbohydrates	43.5g
Protein	10.5g
Fat	46.4g
Fibre	7g
Sugar	4.5g

NOTE: Excluding the toppings

Carrot pakoras with coriander chutney ⓥ

PREP TIME	20 mins
COOK TIME	25 mins
SERVES	4

PAKORAS
1 large carrot, grated
1 small potato, grated
2½cm (1 inch) piece of fresh ginger,
    peeled and grated
2 garlic cloves, crushed
1 tsp salt
½ tsp ground turmeric
1 tsp onion powder
½ green chilli, finely chopped
handful of fresh coriander leaves,
    chopped
75g (2½oz) gram (chickpea) flour
drizzle of olive oil

CORIANDER CHUTNEY
30g (1oz) fresh mint leaves
100g (3½oz) fresh coriander leaves
2.5cm (1 inch) piece of fresh ginger,
    peeled and grated
juice of ½ lemon
1 green chilli
1 tbsp sugar
½ tsp salt
4 tbsp water, plus extra as needed
1 tbsp olive oil

1— Preheat the oven to 200°C (400°F),
    Gas Mark 6 and line a baking
    tray with parchment paper.

2— Add all the pakora ingredients
    into a mixing bowl, except the
    chickpea flour and olive oil,
    and mix well.

3— Sift the chickpea flour on top
    of the ingredients in the bowl.

4— Using your hands, mix all the
    ingredients together thoroughly.
    If the mixture is too wet, you can
    slowly add more chickpea flour.
    The mixture should not be a
    batter but should stick into balls
    with your hands.

5— Using a tablespoon, place
    palm-sized scoops of the
    mixture on the prepared tray.
    Drizzle with olive oil.

6— Bake for about 25 minutes,
    or until golden and crispy.

7— Meanwhile, make the coriander
    chutney. Wash the mint and
    coriander leaves, then drain well.
    Add to a blender with the remaining
    ingredients and blend, stopping
    to scrape down ingredients
    toward the blade. Do not
    blend for too long, otherwise
    it will become very dark.If
    necessary, add more water,
    1 tbsp at a time, until you reach
    your desired consistency.

NUTRITIONAL INFORMATION

Calories	96kcal
Carbohydrates	10.9g
Protein	1.6g
Fat	5.4g
Fibre	2g
Sugar	4.2g

Note— This chutney will
keep in an airtight jar for up
to 1 week in the refrigerator
and frozen for up to 3 months.
You can enjoy it spread on
sandwiches, as a dip, dressing
or drizzled on chaat.

Spicy and sweet nuts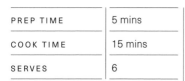

PREP TIME	5 mins
COOK TIME	15 mins
SERVES	6

400g (14oz) mixed nuts
   (almonds, cashews,
   pistachios)
100g (3½oz) pumpkin seeds
2 tbsp finely chopped
   fresh rosemary
2 tbsp maple syrup
   (or honey if not vegan)
1 tbsp sunflower oil
2 tsp sea salt flakes
¼ tsp cayenne pepper

1— Preheat the oven to 160°C (325°F), Gas Mark 3. Line a large rimmed baking sheet with parchment paper.

2— Tip the nuts and pumpkin seeds onto the sheet and set it aside.

3— In a small bowl, combine the rosemary, maple syrup, oil, salt and cayenne. Mix until blended.

4— Pour the mixture over the nuts and stir well until all of the nuts are lightly coated. Spread the mixture in a single layer across the sheet.

5— Bake, stirring after the first 10 minutes and then every 5 minutes thereafter, until almost no maple syrup remains on the parchment paper and the nuts are deeply golden, about 15 minutes.

NUTRITIONAL INFORMATION

Calories	527kcal
Carbohydrates	23.3g
Protein	16.6g
Fat	44.9g
Fibre	7.1g
Sugar	7.4g

No-bake banana blondies

PREP TIME	10 mins
CHILLING TIME	2 hours
SERVES	6

1 large banana, mashed
90g (3¼oz) oat flour (just blitz
    your rolled oats, you may
    possibly need extra)
60g (2¼oz) peanut butter
    (or your nut butter of choice)
80g (2¾oz) maple syrup, agave
    syrup or honey
2 tbsp dark chocolate chips

1— In a large mixing bowl combine the mashed banana, oat flour, peanut butter and maple syrup. Mix well until all the ingredients are combined.

2— Transfer to a parchment-lined 23cm (9 inch) square tin or container.

3— Press the mixture to make sure it's tightly packed, then top with the chocolate chips and press them down gently into the mixture.

4— Put in the fridge for 2 hours. Cut into 6 squares and enjoy.

NUTRITIONAL INFORMATION

Calories	193kcal
Carbohydrates	28.6g
Protein	4.8g
Fat	7.7g
Fibre	3.2g
Sugar	14g

Trail mix popcorn ⓥ

PREP TIME	2 mins
COOK TIME	5 mins
SERVES	6

POPCORN
2 tbsp coconut oil
20g (¾oz) popcorn kernels
pinch of salt

TRAIL MIX
25g (1oz) your favourite cereal
   or granola
25g (1oz) raw pecans
25g (1oz) raw almonds
25g (1oz) dark chocolate chips
   or pieces
25g (1oz) freeze-dried raspberries
   or any other dried fruit, such
   as mangoes, apples or
   pineapples

1— Heat the coconut oil in a large saucepan over a medium–high heat.

2— Put three popcorn kernels into the oil and cover the pan.

3— When the kernels pop, add the rest of the popcorn kernels in an even layer. Cover and remove from heat, then count to 20 seconds.

4— Return the pan to the heat with the lid slightly ajar. Once the popping starts, gently shake the pan by moving it back and forth.

5— Once you hear the popping slow to 2 or 3 seconds between pops, remove the pan from the heat and transfer the popcorn to a large serving bowl.

6— Sprinkle with salt and let the popcorn cool.

7— Once cool, add all the trail mix ingredients and mix well. Store in airtight jars for 1 week and portion out for snacks as desired.

NUTRITIONAL INFORMATION

Calories	161kcal
Carbohydrates	12.9g
Protein	2.7g
Fat	11.7g
Fibre	3.1g
Sugar	3.6g

Chapter 6

Indulgent puddings

Fool everyone with these tempting puddings that are made from nutritious and healthy ingredients. If you're looking for a quick sweet fix, you'll find exactly what you need here.

Raspberry Eton mess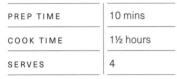

PREP TIME	10 mins
COOK TIME	1½ hours
SERVES	4

drained liquid from a 400g (14oz)
    can of chickpeas (aquafaba)
100g (3½oz) golden caster sugar
200g (7oz) raspberries
1 tsp rosewater
400g (14oz) coconut yogurt

TOPPINGS (OPTIONAL)
dried rose petals
handful of crushed pistachios

1— Preheat the oven to 110°C (225°F), Gas Mark ¼ and line a baking tray with parchment paper.

2— Whisk the drained chickpea liquid with an electric whisk until white, fluffy and holding its shape (this will take a few minutes).

3— Gradually whisk in the caster sugar until your aquafaba meringue forms stiff peaks.

4— Spoon the meringue onto the baking tray and bake for 1½ hours or until firm. Switch off the heat and leave in the oven until completely cool.

5— Blitz most of the raspberries in a blender with the rosewater until smooth.

6— Put the coconut yogurt in a large bowl. Gently stir through half of the raspberry purée, rippling it through the yogurt.

7— Layer the raspberry yogurt mixture into dessert glasses with crushed meringue and the remaining raspberry purée.

8— Sprinkle with some dried rose petals and crushed pistachios, if using, and the remaining fresh raspberries.

NUTRITIONAL INFORMATION

Calories	173kcal
Carbohydrates	28.1g
Protein	2.5g
Fat	5.7g
Fibre	2.1g
Sugar	24.6g

NOTE: Excluding the toppings

Berry crumble ⓥ

PREP TIME	5 mins
COOK TIME	35 mins
SERVES	4

CRUMBLE
50g (1¾oz) almond flour
80g (2¾oz) rolled oats
½ tsp salt
70g (2½oz) peanut butter
(or any nut butter)
70g (2½oz) maple or agave syrup
(or honey if not vegan)

FILLING
450g (1lb) strawberries and
blueberries (or berries of
your choice), fresh or frozen
1 tbsp maple syrup
juice of ½ lemon

1— Preheat the oven to 180°C (350°F), Gas Mark 4 and line a 20cm (8 inch) baking tin with parchment paper.

2— Put all the filling ingredients into a large bowl and mix well, then spread this mixture evenly across the bottom of your baking tin.

3— In the same bowl (no need to wash), stir the crumble ingredients together until there are no dry clumps left.

4— Use your hands to crumble the dough over the top of the berry mixture.

5— Bake for 30–35 minutes, or until the crumb is crisp and slightly browned.

NUTRITIONAL INFORMATION

Calories	351 kcal
Carbohydrates	46.8g
Protein	10g
Fat	16.5g
Fibre	7.5g
Sugar	23g

Note — If you used frozen fruit instead of fresh, you may need an extra 5–10 minutes in the oven, as it has more moisture.

Indulgent chocolate dip ⓥ

PREP TIME	5 mins
SOAKING TIME	1 hour
SERVES	10

150g (5½oz) cashews
80g (2¾oz) maple syrup
2 tbsp cocoa powder
2 tsp coconut oil, melted
¼ tsp vanilla extract

TOPPINGS (OPTIONAL)
chopped dark chocolate
assorted fruits
crackers
marshmallows
popcorn

1— Put the cashews in a bowl and cover with warm water. Let them soak for at least 1 hour.

2— Rinse the cashews, tip into a high-powered blender and blend until smooth.

3— Add the remaining ingredients to the blender and blend until smooth and creamy. If the mixture is too thick, add some cold water, a teaspoon at a time, until you get your desired consistency.

4— Pour the dip into a bowl and top with some chopped chocolate, assorted fruits, crackers, marshmallows, popcorn or whatever you fancy.

NUTRITIONAL INFORMATION

Calories	110kcal
Carbohydrates	10.5g
Protein	2.9g
Fat	7.1g
Fibre	0.8g
Sugar	5.7g

NOTE: Excluding the toppings

Pineapple and coconut sorbet

PREP TIME	10 mins
FREEZING TIME	8 hours
SERVES	6

1 pineapple, peeled, cored and cut
   into 2cm (¾ inch) chunks
400ml (14fl oz) coconut cream
2 tbsp maple or agave syrup (or
   honey if not vegan)
handful of toasted coconut flakes

1— Put the pineapple into a blender along with the coconut cream and maple syrup. Blend until smooth.

2— Pour into a deep container, cover and place in the freezer for 4 hours or until slushy, but not totally frozen.

3— Remove from the freezer, whisk using an electric whisk or hand whisk, then return to the freezer for another 4 hours, or until fully set.

4— Serve with the toasted coconut flakes.

NUTRITIONAL INFORMATION

Calories	255kcal
Carbohydrates	22.1g
Protein	3.5g
Fat	8.2g
Fibre	4.3g
Sugar	32.9g

5-minute coffee pots

PREP TIME	5 mins
SETTING TIME	2 hours
SERVES	4

2 tsp coffee granules
1 tbsp boiling water
100g (3½oz) dates
2 tbsp cocoa powder
350g (12oz) silken tofu, drained
pinch of sea salt flakes

TOPPINGS (OPTIONAL)
crushed dark chocolate
crushed nuts

1— Dissolve the coffee granules in the boiling water and mix to a paste.

2— Put the dates, cocoa powder and coffee paste into a blender or food processor and blend until they have formed a smooth paste.

3— Add the tofu to the processor and blend further until the mixture is completely smooth.

4— Spoon into four ramekins and place in the fridge. Refrigerate for at least 2 hours until set.

5— Serve straight from the fridge, sprinkled with sea salt flakes, crushed chocolate and nuts, if using.

NUTRITIONAL INFORMATION

Calories	133kcal
Carbohydrates	23.9g
Protein	5.8g
Fat	3.1g
Fibre	2.5g
Sugar	17.9g

NOTE: Excluding the toppings

Note — If the dates aren't moist, soak in hot water for 10 minutes to soften and then drain and use.

Blueberries

USES

Add a handful to porridge, granola, muffins and flapjacks. Use to top thick yogurt or to add a little sweetness and pack an antioxidant punch to smoothies. Delicious with anything chocolate, especially the darker varieties – think 70–85 per cent cocoa solids.

Blueberries are classed as a 'superfood' because they are nutrient dense and provide high levels of essential vitamins (C and K especially) and minerals such as manganese. They are also a good source of fibre and water and are low in fat and sugar, meaning both their glycaemic index and glycaemic load are low –particularly good news for anyone trying to lose weight, as well as for managing diabetes.

An added benefit of eating blueberries is that they are high in antioxidants, notably anthocyanins, which are responsible for the deep purple/pink or red colours of some fruit and veg. Regular intake of antioxidants is vital as they protect the body from free-radical damage and oxidative stress, both of which can lead to diseases, including cancers caused by cell and DNA damage. Oxidative stress speeds up the brain's ageing process, so a daily dose of these little purple berries is a great way to nurture your grey matter! Antioxidants also contribute to a healthy cardiovascular system by helping to reduce oxidized cholesterol in the body – one of the biggest risk factors in heart health.

Equally beneficial, the antioxidant and vitamin C content of blueberries boosts the immune system, while vitamin C is also needed to make collagen, a protein that helps wounds to heal and keeps the skin elastic.

Gooey chocolate pudding

PREP TIME	5 mins
COOK TIME	15 mins
SERVES	2

3 tbsp ground almonds
2 tbsp cacao powder
½ tsp baking powder
1½ tbsp maple syrup
3 tbsp oat milk
   (or your milk of choice)
1 tsp coconut oil, melted
pinch of salt

1— Preheat the oven to 180°C (350°F), Gas Mark 4.

2— Tip the dry ingredients into a small bowl and stir to combine. Add the maple syrup, oat milk and coconut oil and whisk until smooth.

3— Pour the mixture into 2 ramekins and bake for 12–14 minutes or until set on the top but still gooey in the centre. Serve warm.

NUTRITIONAL INFORMATION

Calories	225kcal
Carbohydrates	19.8g
Protein	6g
Fat	15g
Fibre	4.6g
Sugar	22.2g

Creamy rice pudding

PREP TIME	5 mins
COOK TIME	1 hour
SERVES	4

75g (2½oz) pudding rice,
4 tbsp maple or agave syrup (or
   honey if not vegan)
1 tsp vanilla extract
½ tsp ground cinnamon
600ml (20fl oz) almond milk
400g (14oz) can of coconut milk

TOPPINGS (OPTIONAL)
handful of crushed pistachios
Warm berry compote
   (see page 20)
toasted coconut flakes

1— Preheat the oven to 180°C (350°F), Gas Mark 4. Grease a medium-sized baking dish.

2— Put all the ingredients in the baking dish and mix well until they are incorporated.

3— Bake in the oven for 1 hour or until the rice is soft. Top with the pistachios, berry compote and coconut flakes, if using.

NUTRITIONAL INFORMATION

Calories	255kcal
Carbohydrates	28.1g
Protein	2.7g
Fat	15.5g
Fibre	0.7g
Sugar	14.9g

NOTES: Excluding the toppings

Chocolate chia pudding with a chocolate shell ⓥ

PREP TIME	15 mins
SOAKING TIME	8 hours
SETTING TIME	30 mins
SERVES	2

CHIA PUDDING
60g (2¼oz) chia seeds
240ml (8fl oz) almond milk
(or your milk of choice)
2 tbsp cocoa powder
1 tbsp maple syrup
1 tsp ground cinnamon

CHOCOLATE SHELL
30g (1oz) dark chocolate
(or your chocolate of choice)
1 tsp coconut oil
handful of crushed peanuts
(optional)

1— Combine all the chia pudding ingredients in a medium bowl. Cover and refrigerate overnight or for at least 8 hours.

2— Transfer the mixture to a high-powered blender and blend until completely smooth. Divide into two small dessert pots.

3— To make the shell, melt your chocolate along with the coconut oil in a microwave, whisking with a fork until smooth.

4— Pour the melted chocolate over the chia puddings and top with the crushed nuts, if using.

5— Refrigerate until set – around 30 minutes.

NUTRITIONAL INFORMATION

Calories	316kcal
Carbohydrates	31g
Protein	9.2g
Fat	20.2g
Fibre	12.5g
Sugar	10.6g

NOTES: Excluding the peanuts

Strawberry and pistachio frozen yogurt + ⓥ

PREP TIME	10 mins
FREEZING TIME	8 hours
SERVES	4

720g (1lb 9oz) full-fat Greek
    yogurt (or your non-dairy
    yogurt of choice)
280g (10oz) frozen strawberries
2 tsp vanilla extract
4 tbsp maple syrup (optional)
100g (3½oz) pistachios, crushed

1— Spoon the yogurt into an ice-cube tray (or mini muffin pan) and freeze for 8 hours or overnight.

2— Put the yogurt ice cubes in a blender with the frozen strawberries, vanilla and maple syrup, if using, until creamy. Stir in the crushed pistachios.

3— Serve immediately or store in the freezer until ready to serve.

NUTRITIONAL INFORMATION

Calories	387kcal
Carbohydrates	37.7g
Protein	12.8g
Fat	22.5g
Fibre	4.5g
Sugar	29g

Note— If you're using a non-dairy yogurt, opt for a higher fat one like coconut, otherwise the frozen yogurt will come out icy.

Top ingredients and their benefits

AUBERGINES
An 80g (2¾oz) serving of aubergine counts toward your five-a-day. Because it is high in fibre and very low in fat and sugar, aubergine is an ideal ingredient to use in a weight management programme and a great option for people who have type 2 diabetes.

BANANAS
Bananas are commonly known to be a great source of potassium, but they also contain a myriad of other vitamins and minerals too. Bananas provide soluble fibre, which helps to lower cholesterol and to maintain a healthy bowel. (The soluble fibre absorbs water in your gut, forming a gel, which slows down digestion, keeping you feeling fuller for longer, and it may also reduce bloating.)

COURGETTES
Courgettes have a high content of water and fibre which helps to soften your stools, making them easier to pass, and lessening your chances of constipation. Courgettes are very low in carbohydrates: 225g (8oz) of cooked courgette contains only 3g of carbs. This combination of high fibre/water and low carbs, can also help to stabilize your blood sugars.

CUCUMBERS
Cucumbers are made up of about 96 per cent water, meaning they're great for hydrating the body and skin. In addition, they are also rich in antioxidants, which play an important role in protecting the cells from damage.

DAIRY AND EQUIVALENTS
Dairy products are the biggest sources of calcium for Western diets. Calcium is a very important mineral as it's the main component for bones and teeth. If you're following a dairy-free diet, it's important to ensure you get the mineral from alternative sources. Check the nutritional information of plant-based milks to make sure they are fortified with calcium. Other great sources of calcium are green leafy vegetables like kale, as well as tofu, fortified breakfast cereals, bread, nuts and seeds.

JACKFRUIT
Jackfruit is a tree fruit found growing in tropical regions across Asia, Africa and South America. Its meaty stringy texture means it is becoming increasingly popular as an alternative to meat. Although jackfruit doesn't provide the same proteins found in meat, it brings other health benefits: it is high in fibre, antioxidants and vitamins A and C. Studies suggest that jackfruit may contain antimicrobial, antifungal and anti-inflammatory properties. You can buy jackfruit canned, frozen or dried in strips.

MANGOES
Mangoes also contain good levels of immune-boosting vitamins A and C. Vitamin C helps to form collagen – the protein that acts as a scaffold to skin, keeping it plump and firm – and vitamin A also plays is part in keeping our skin and hair healthy. There is some evidence that it can protect against the signs of ageing.

MUSHROOMS
Mushrooms are the only non-animal source of vitamin D, making them invaluable for vegans and vegetarians. As mushrooms grow, they are exposed to ultraviolet radiation, either from sunlight or a UV lamp, which increases their vitamin D concentration. When you buy fresh mushrooms, leave them in direct sunlight for 20 minutes before eating – this simple act increases the amount of vitamin D they contain and a serving can provide 50–100 per cent of your daily requirement.

OATS
Oats are wholegrains – those contain all parts of the grain: the bran, endosperm and germ. Most of the goodness is found in the outer bran layer and the inner germ. When any grains are processed to make white pasta, biscuits or white bread, the bran and germ portions are removed along with the goodness. Oats provide: fibre, B vitamins and folic acid, essential fatty acids (omega-3 fats), protein and antioxidants, including vitamin E and selenium.

PEANUT BUTTER
Peanut butter may be high in fat and calories, but it contains mostly unsaturated fats, which are the healthy type. Peanuts are a great source of protein, helping you stay satisfied for longer. Always check the labels of your peanut butter as you want to buy one that hasn't been highly processed with sugar, salt or palm oils.

PEAS

Peas are very high in protein: 100g (3½oz) of peas provides more protein than 40g (1½oz) of almonds or a tablespoon of peanut butter. There is very little difference between fresh and frozen peas, making frozen a useful and cost-effective alternative.

POPCORN

Popcorn is low in fat, high in fibre and naturally gluten-free, so it can be a healthy snack, depending on the other ingredients added in. Shop-bought popcorn has usually been cooked in butter, salt or sugar, so offsetting the nutritional content. It is therefore always best to make your own popcorn as you can control exactly what you put in it.

POTATO PEELINGS

Can you believe that potato skins have more nutritional benefit than the actual potato? Not only are they loaded with fibre (four times as much as a whole potato), but also vitamins B and C. The B group of vitamins provide the body with the energy needed for numerous functions involving the nerves, muscles, skin, heart and brain.

RED CABBAGE

Red cabbage is high in antioxidants, namely anthocyanins, as well as potassium, folate and vitamin C.

SPINACH

Spinach is rich in iron: 100g (3½oz) of raw spinach contains 2.71mg of iron, which is 19 per cent of the recommended daily allowance. This mineral plays a central role in the function of red blood cells, which help transport oxygen around the body and supports energy production. Your body absorbs iron from plant sources better when you eat it with foods that are high in vitamin C, like citrus fruits.

STRAWBERRIES

The most abundant micronutrients in strawberries are: vitamin C – necessary for immune and skin health; manganese – important for many processes in the body; and potassium – essential to regulate blood pressure. Strawberries also have a low glycaemic index, so they avoid those big spikes in sugar.

SWEETCORN

There are lots of myths claiming sweetcorn has no nutritional benefits, but this couldn't be further from the truth. Sweetcorn is a wholegrain that is very high in fibre and in folate too. Folate contributes to the formation of healthy red blood cells, and to the baby's development in the womb. The recommended daily intake of vitamin B9 is 200 micrograms, and you can get 35 micrograms with just a 100g (3½oz) portion of sweetcorn.

SWEET POTATOES

Sweet potatoes are packed full of beta carotene, a substance that is used by the body to make more vitamin A. This vitamin, also known as retinol, is important for normal vision, the immune system and reproduction.

TOFU

Tofu is simply coagulated soya milk. It is rich in protein and high in isoflavones, compounds that are produced by legumes. Isoflavones provide some key benefits: they are often termed 'phytoestrogens' because they mimic a weak form of the hormone oestrogen and some women find it aids their menopausal symptoms, like hot flushes. In addition, eating food rich in isoflavones, such as beans, lentils and peas, has been found to reduce levels of 'bad' cholesterol. Finally, these compounds are also a great source of protective antioxidants.

TOMATOES

Not only are tomatoes a great source of vitamins C, K and A, they are also a great source of beta carotene, which has been shown to help reduce UV damage from over-exposure to the sun. (This doesn't mean that eating lots of tomatoes will protect you from sunburn, so you should still follow guidelines to prevent this.) Cooking tomatoes actually boosts their nutritional value.

TURMERIC

The main active ingredient in turmeric is curcumin, which contributes significantly to the health benefits of incorporating this root (fresh or powdered) in the diet. There is evidence that turmeric helps reduce inflammation within the body, for example in joint arthritis. Curcumin can also help support gut health, including relieving excess gas, abdominal pain and bloating.

Index

Acknowledgements

I have to start by thanking my wonderful husband Naveen. Without him, there would be no Doctor Bowl. He was the one who pushed me to start my Instagram page and has continued to support and motivate me to be the best version of myself. Whilst I was recipe testing for this book, he looked after Anoushka, and always cleaned up the aftermath in the kitchen!

A massive thank you to the team at Kyle Books, especially Louise McKeever, who trusted me with my vision for this book.

Cara Cormack and Saskia Sidey – thank you for the wonderful photography and food styling. We created some great memories together, and I've learnt so much from you all.

Thank you to my wonderful parents and siblings for your endless support and encouragement.

Thank you to my best friend Almas, who has always managed to make me smile at times of stress

And finally, a huge thank you to my amazing social media followers. You've given me some life-changing opportunities, and I am forever grateful to you all.